What people are :

The Afterlife, a journey to

The Afterlife, a journey to will provide comfort and hope to anyone who has lost a loved one and is questioning whether their loved one is still safe and provided for. With compassion and insight, Stephen provides possible explanations to some of the most challenging questions about the Afterlife.
Dr. Matthew Welsh, Founder of Spiritual Media Blog

This book enthralled me: in it I travelled with characters who found themselves experiencing the agony caused to others by their actions during their lifetime, and with those who had created and were locked into their own pain. While reading I had to discipline myself not to have a quick look at the end of the book to find out if there would be happy endings, until I recognised the theme of love that was guiding and supporting every character in a pathway leading to their respite or healing. A truly beautiful book.
Annabel Muis, Reiki Master and coauthor of *Turning Points: Regaining Joy after Loss*

There are many chronicles of the lives of those who have traversed the dimensions of existence that are said to be 'the Spiritual Path'. There are also countless stories of those who have experienced 'Near Death Experiences' and give us glimpses of that which awaits us after our transition from life. However, there are few who have brought to us details of the dimensions and path 'on the other side'.

The Afterlife is one of those few. In a language both poetic and evocative, it takes us through the soul's journey through the dimensions of purification to its fruition of service to life.
The Universal Storyteller, Divine at Play

The Afterlife is an evocative and challenging journey through an ethereal realm in a quest for enlightenment and understanding. Chong takes us to the spiritual precipice and beyond in this perceptive and visionary interpretation of another world.
John Singe, author of *My Island Home, Coral Sea Story* and *Blackbird Story*

Whatever your thoughts and beliefs are about what happens immediately after death, our one inevitable destiny, Stephen Chong's book entitled *The Afterlife* will give you some thought-provoking insights into his understanding. His appreciation of truth and consequences are not to be discarded easily, and one hopes his interpretation is somewhere close, as it is far more comforting than some of the models of yore. A great read.
Chris Shaw, author of *The Imposter* and *Counterpunch*

The Afterlife is an intense, mystical, and ethereal journey into heaven and our purification into 'Divine Love' in our Afterlife. It stirs an examination of our conscience – to better prepare for our Afterlife. We will be accountable for what we have done and what we have failed to do.
Mario Calanna, Calanna Pharmacies, author of *Design a Good Life*

Richly descriptive. Beautifully written. Takes us on a journey that we could never imagine.
Dr. E.M. Martin, author of *Journey Beyond the Self*

Stephen Chong's evocative style and writing and how the words weave a magical web is both enthralling and delightful. I have loved all of Stephen's books and this one is no exception – it is profoundly beautiful with a great message of hope.
Grace Angel Forest, North Queensland, Australia

Stephen Chong is a writer who moves with the divine compelling him to release what he sees into poetic and sincere words. This book is a reflection of his call to be a writer that leaves the reader awestruck, evoked and jettisoned into a new way of thinking and even loving. Stephen encourages all towards an inspirational world understanding how "each... is a teardrop from the eyes of our Father".
Letizia C. De Rosa, JCU Special Collections: DEROSA Collections

Your best one yet.
Mark Ruge, Reiki Master, www.markruge.com.au

The Afterlife is a guide to the hereafter and what awaits us all after we die. It touches on heaven's various realms and portals that one will journey through after the inevitable 'end'. However, there is no real end to life as we only begin a new journey after our time on Earth. Athar, the narrator, takes us on a journey through the afterlife and shares the details and secrets that lie just out of reach. Every human being has access to this information; however, most are just unable to tap into it.

The Afterlife is an interesting and thought-provoking book that seeks to enlighten and bring spiritual awakening to the reader. This book is written as both a guide and a story that explains the journey every human being will find themselves taking after death. We all must face the crossing and discover what our life on earth amounted to. I thought this book was very well written and, honestly, I found it extremely absorbing. As someone who was raised within the Christian faith, it was deeply moving and engrossing. It challenges what you as a person believe and also challenges your faith. Overall, this book was wonderfully written and I think it has a lot to offer readers in terms of spirituality. I would recommend this book as it gives the reader food for thought.
Miche Arendse, Readers' Favorite

Books By Stephen Chong M.Ed.

The Book of Testaments: A Practical Guide for Spiritual
Realisation
ISBN: 9781921555350

The Music of the Soul: A Pathway to a Rich and Fulfilling Life
ISBN: 9781921829185

Letters Across Time: A journey of enlightenment
ISBN: 9781782790181

The Power and the Possible: A Teenager's Traverse of the
World
ISBN: 9780994304933

Bodies of Consequence
ISBN: 9780648457909

Feature Film Screenplays

Bodies of Consequence
A Meaningful Life
The Power and the Possible
Mean Paradise
The Pivot Point

For more information on Stephen Chong M.Ed. and his books,
visit his website at www.stephenchong.com.au

The Afterlife,
a journey to

Now you know what will happen

The Afterlife, a journey to

Now you know what will happen

Stephen Chong M.Ed.

6TH
BOOKS

Winchester, UK
Washington, USA

JOHN HUNT PUBLISHING

First published by Sixth Books, 2023
Sixth Books is an imprint of John Hunt Publishing Ltd., No. 3 East St., Alresford,
Hampshire SO24 9EE, UK
office@jhpbooks.com
www.johnhuntpublishing.com
www.6th-books.com

For distributor details and how to order please visit the 'Ordering' section on our website.

Text copyright: Stephen Chong 2021

ISBN: 978 1 80341 151 4
978 1 80341 152 1 (ebook)
Library of Congress Control Number: 2021925067

A CIP catalogue record for this book is available from the British Library.

Design: Stuart Davies

UK: Printed and bound by CPI Group (UK) Ltd, Croydon, CR0 4YY
Printed in North America by CPI GPS partners

We operate a distinctive and ethical publishing philosophy in
all areas of our business, from our global network of authors to
production and worldwide distribution.

Contents

Acknowledgements

If ever there was a time to thank my guardian angels, this would be it. Then again, I know they are with me all the time, so it seems rather trite to thank them all the time. Yet, this I must do, for without them this book would not have been written. The constant urges to write not knowing what I was going to write has much to do with their ever-present flow of the grand visions, prose and words given to my fingers to type.

Nor would this book exist without the perpetual love of family. I now fully understand the story of *Samson & Delilah*. By cutting his hair Samson was sapped of his strength... In my case, my family is my hair... Please don't cut my hair!

Prologue

Finding out about the afterlife teaches us how to live.
S.P. Chong (2021)

My name is Athar. At least it is now. That is, now that I'm here, in heaven. I can only tell you the story now, I couldn't back then. Back then it was too painful, it hurt too much. But now I know. Now I know what happens. But more than that, I now know why. Yet, I am not here to tell you what to believe, only to tell you what is true.

Is there life after death? Surely this must be the most consummate question one could ask. After all, we are all going to die. Imagine that each of the 7.7 billion-odd people currently above terra firma will at some stage not be above it. The perennial question is, "When, not if?" The following question is, "What then?" Is that all there is? Is it just a case of, "That'it!"? We go to dust and all that is left are legacies of a life lived well – or otherwise. Leaving those we leave behind to deal with the grief of loss and memories of love, passion and/or harsh recollections.

To describe what happens to us in the afterlife requires a complete and total leap of faith. It is not just a case of an indomitable need to know what happens. Nor is it cloaked in the desire to reassure ourselves that we do not just revert to a pile of dust after many years of struggle and toil. The search for knowledge and truth of what lies beyond is far more direct. It is, at its most fundamental, a task that will bring light to a better life. It will illuminate the actions and meaning behind what we do with our lives, and more particularly, how we do it.

The quest to understand 'life after death' becomes then a precursor to taking the next step (in life). How can I make life better? What do I have to do to make life a happier, more fulfilling place – one less inclined to a contest? If I know to take the right actions NOW, then what becomes consequential is the 'reward' in the life hereafter. Whatever that 'reward' may be.

My quest in this book is not to answer the question, "Is there life after death?" For me, the answer to the question is an emphatic, "YES." More to the point, my aim in this book is to describe what happens. To take you on a journey into the next realm, to show you what awaits. To describe as vividly as I can, the events and laws that govern the consequences of life, and life after death.

But where do we go for such enlightenment? After all, we are not 'dead' yet. How do we know what happens?

There are, of course, numerous mediums who might bridge the great divide between us here on earth and those that have departed. Those mediums of pure heart play an important role to connect those seeking, with those (on the other side) willing to make the connection. Love is generally the bond in such regard. Because of our enduring love for another, we cherish knowledge of their continued well-being, their continued existence even. To know that someone we love remains eternal is a blessing beyond imagining. It gives us hope and prolongs cherished memories, unfinished business, or unspoken words of love that before could not be expressed.

This book that you hold in your palms is not like those that have preceded it. It does not require the intermediary of someone who may intercede and call upon departed spirits. It does not pretend to be written by a discarnate spirit of the nether world who has come to tell of fortune or prediction. This book is written by my hand and firmly grasps the true nature of who I am. I, as you are, am a being of the divine. I connect with that which I AM. To communicate directly with my HIGHER self and know that he speaks to me as plainly as I speak to you.

This does not make me special. This is not a gift for the select few. The ability and wherewithal to connect to our HIGHER

SELF is available to us all. Yet, I cannot prove to you what I know; I can only share my experience with you. My fervent desire is to describe for you 'what happens to us when we die'. This is not to give you comfort for that which will come to pass for us all. Rather, it is to give you the keys to a life that will provide you with hope and guidance. Sustain you in the knowledge that you are a being of the divine. After all, you are an eternal teardrop of the grace of God, our Creator. As part of this grand design, we each have our creed, community, beliefs and family. We each have been subject to the pressures of pain, suffering, problems and temptations. None of us could ever be placed under the banner of 'perfect'. Yet, each of us, in our way, seeks an explanation as to, why? Why has life been so hard? Why did I have to suffer so?

I do not come to you to proclaim myself as a healer, nor medium, nor even a mystic. Rather, I do say to you that what I know, all can know. The HIGHER SELF that I have come to know is no more absent from you than your skin. Oneness with your HIGHER SELF is never absent – it is the listening that is often intermittent, or in need of reparation.

Within this tome I give you the wherewithal to know the truth of what lies beyond the great veil. For, ultimately, the cause of our evolution is in this earthly life, the effect is in the eternal and unavoidable life of spirit.

It is, as spoken by the great Master,

If ye abide in me, and my words abide in you, ye shall ask what you will, and it shall be done unto you.
John XV:7

With the tome you now hold to your hands, I can only lay claim to the words as the author by virtue that it is my fingers that are waltzing on the keyboard. The source of the words is what you, the reader, need to determine as truth, folly or fiction. I guess it comes down to the ism of 'What you believe is true', given the subject of this book, namely, 'The Afterlife' – what happens to us after we die? Burdens of proof as often demanded by enquiring minds are difficult to provide when in consideration of things ephemeral and/or spiritual.

In consideration therefore of your system of belief – whether you are agnostic, atheist or a true believer of traditional religious ideology – it matters not. I ask only that you approach the following pages with a mind open to possibilities. With a heart bursting to know the truth and an eye to reveal the truest expression of what you will take from this reading, to make your life, and lives of those you love, a grander, more expansive expression of a life well-lived. To be able to say upon your last breath that, "I have done my best," "I have left nothing behind on the field of play," and that, "I carry no regrets to the Afterlife that awaits me," is all to which a humble author could aspire.

May *The Afterlife* work its magic at whatever level for you, and let it inspire you to achieve great things in your life. Once worked, use this knowledge as your inspiration and motivation. Indeed, you could read the 'stories' again and again, each time extracting a different message or meaning. This is YOUR journey of discovery.

Let us therefore proceed upon this journey, you and I, with the surety of eternal wisdom beyond anything else ever known...

Love is stronger than death.

Let us begin, therefore, by encapsulating this journey through the gift of prose:

Behold! I am your God Almighty.
It is from me that from all life springs, and to whom all life returns,

But you must know that everything is life.

Do not be afraid, for I am not a judgemental God – this is the design of men who know not the truth.

Yet, it is a return to innocence that will be your most profound journey of life.

All who are innocent are the truest reflection of God on earth. Your children, your elderly and your sick will all return to me as true children of God, I AM.

Fear not for the departed, for they reside with me, as me, and know also that they reside in you, as you, for we are not separate – all are one in the spirit that I AM.

Seek all that you love in the silence where I, and they, will be found.

Call my name and I will be with you; call their name and they will be with you.

Love is your bond, and to love you will all return, for love is what I AM.

Excerpt from *Letters Across Time* (Chong, 2013, 191)

Chapter One

The Passage

Eternity's mirror laid bare,
Neither saint, nor spectre reposed from reveal.
Freedom's choice removed from soiled hands –
Nay, I say to deeds exposed to inevitable truth.

Would thou'st weep words to succour?
Revealed to truth shall thy deeds be.
That thou art cleaved by laws known, or closed to eye,
Nay, I say to heart pierced with regret and insouciance.

Dirge and mournful wailing,
Pain and suffering caused to regret.
That thou art one like the other,
What thou has sown, to see it reaped, stands unbroken.

A pathway unique, steps devoid of choice,
Robes befit fit the king, and the pauper of spirit.
Would thou'st leave me alone to such fate, oh, lord of hosts?
Nay, for love's tendrils shine to find redemption within.

The bishop's day, as usual, had been filled with the many and multi-varied facets of administration of his See. *All according to God's will amongst his many believers,* he thought – but he was tired. It was more often that he was feeling the weight of his years in his bones. In limited spare moments of divine reflection, he was beginning to see the expanse of his remaining days in moments, rather than the years before him. *There is much to be done,* he mused, as he sighed deeply while removing his vestments to seek the comfort and warmth of his bed. Only then did he notice the deepening darkness of the rings under his eyes as he passed by the looking glass.

Sleep came only with a struggle. It was as if his need to sleep conflicted with his desire for peace. His dreamscape was filled with the chorale of a thousand voices crying in unified pain and suffering. It was discordant music that filled the essence of his nightly spirit with dread. Even in sleep, tears managed to seep from his eyes from his poorly constructed REM. Yet, he awakened with a start only to wonder why his cheeks were wet.

Rousing with a jolt, he felt chilled air streaming through the open window of his chamber. The gelid wind made the drapes sway in a silent apparition. *I'm sure I closed the window before going to bed*, he thought, as he threw back the blankets to rise and seal the opened portal to the outer world. His involuntary shudder when reaching to pull the window shut only reminded him to be more aware before going to bed. Despite the chill, he stood a moment, quietly in awe of the full moon, and silent flight of what appeared to be a large owl swooping around the trees just on the perimeter of his ornate garden. The "Hoot, Hoot" of the owl sent another unbidden tingle down his spine. He seemed to remember reading something about an owl's portent for wisdom, or was it a harbinger of death? He couldn't remember which.

Despite the now firmly closed window, he tugged at the length of his bedclothes to avert the chill in his bones. It was then that he saw it from the corner of his eye, just as he turned to return to the warmth of his bed. Dark, with menacing eyes all lit up with red peril known only to another dimension. The black hood and flowing robe enveloping the otherworldly figure confirmed only that the fear that had arisen in the bishop's chest was eminently tangible. He felt his heart turn to icicles when he noticed that the scythe held in the spectre's left hand was even taller than its bearer.

The tic in his left eye, the one that he did most days exert influence over, flickered like it was on steroids, and he could feel his body tremble without volition before this unbidden manifestation from across the ethers. A soundless scream found a way to his strangled vocal cords, and he could do little to control the trembling of his chin. Then a stolen glance at his mitre, placed strategically on his desk beside the wall, reminded him who he was, or at least what his title was. It succeeded little as he tried his best to straighten his spine and project a modicum of gravitas.

"Who, who are you?" was all the bishop could stammer as he leaned toward his side dresser for support.

The being merely lifted the bones of its right hand to point directly at the man of God.

"It is time. You must come," was the only reply from a guttural depth, as if the words were wrenched from a furnace pit of black ooze.

The bishop's mouth fell agape, and he pleaded with his eyes, trying to force words through his strangled vocals.

"Do you mean that death is upon me, and I go to heaven?"

The otherworldly being did not reply, merely stood silent, eyes aglow and fixed to its purpose.

A few eternal heartbeats passed as the bishop's eyes then fired with growing realisation.

"I'm going home – to God," he said in confirmation to his inner-urgings. "I am to be welcomed at the Gates by the Holy Hosts. My life as Bishop has seen me to the portals of heaven."

Again, the guttural voice resonated like a thousand drumbeats of thunder.

"Bishop, you are a long way from home," said the Reaper as he stepped closer to the still trembling man.

"But I don't understand. I am a man of God. I have been His voice and hand as Bishop of my See. How can it be? I have brought many souls to His door. Given redemption to His flock..."

The reaper said nothing more, merely extended its bony index finger to touch the bishop fully between his terror-filled eyes. Suddenly his mind filled with a blinding light. He reeled backwards as a thousand images poured into his being, as a panorama in a moment describing a lifetime. With a slackened jaw and crumpled visage, tears exploded from the bishop's eyes to flow in a cascade down his cheeks. Then, of the million images that etched across his soul, one seemed to repeat itself ad nauseam. "What have I done? What have I done?" he cried in abandon to heaven and a fate now uncertain, but surely eternal.

The thunder-drum of a thousand voices surrounded him in a cacophony of agony as they cried out in unison of pain and lifetimes of suffering. "Why? Why did you say nothing? Why did you not protect us? How could you condone the abuse? You are a fraud! You are a liar! You knew! You knew!"

Later, after the morning sun had pierced the darkness of the dawn, an urgent knocking came pounding on the door of the bishop's bedroom. *It is most unlike Bishop to sleep through morning prayers*, thought the young acolyte, as he slowly pushed on the door of his master's chamber. The squeak of the hinges did little to calm the lad's trembling poplars.

"Your grace, are you awake?" he asked with hesitation.

Peering around the open portal, with mouth agape and eyes agog, he saw the bishop lying prone on the floor of the bedroom, bedclothes in disarray. Despite the tenderness of his years, he knew his bishop was dead, but certain to his fate in heaven.

"Oh, dear God," he whispered as his heart filled to the brim, then dropped to the floor as a weighted stone.

Being a child of God, and before raising the alarm, the novice mouthed a silent prayer for the departed and made the blessed sign of the cross. It was all he knew how to do at this innocent age, and he prayed hard that it was enough.

For a brief moment, the tunnel of intense light made him wince, but he remembered his readings and how the transition was always made. Although now, right at this precise moment, his hesitation made him feel like his welcome had long disappeared. For where the bishop now found himself could not be fathomed. The mists clung to his being like cloy. It was as if he were being compelled forward towards a destination unknown, without any sense of direction or purpose. The only thing he could discern was the sound of choral voices – at a distance, yet so near he could feel them beat in his core. He managed only to trudge forward, each step releasing another bead of sweat to a brow deeply furrowed at the reality of his current dilemma. But he knew, deep down, wherever he was, he couldn't go back – even if he tried.

Suddenly the mists parted. They were all there, every each one of them. He didn't know who they were. At least he couldn't remember them by name, but he knew why they were here. The crescendo of voices pierced his soul to its fundamental. "You knew, you knew, yet you did nothing," they spat in a chorale.

As if the words were not astringent enough, the chorus of voices in harmony was sufficient to grip his heart in a vice-like clasp. "Aagh, the pain!" he gasped. He could feel their misery and suffering as if it were his own. It felt like the very essence of his soul was being wrenched from his inside to his out.

Without warning one of the many stepped forward, soundless, with hand outstretched seeking his own. Yet it was the young boy's eyes, his vivid blue eyes, that caused the bishop to wince. He could not resist, although deep down he really wanted to. He wanted to be anywhere else but here. He had to take the offered hand – no choice. It instantly transported him to the scene:

The mournful wailing was the first thing the bishop heard as he traversed the downward spiral of the decrepit tunnel. Through the opaque light, he could barely discern the large forbidding door before him. Yet, weeping and lament were emanating from whatever lay behind this portal to hades. He had to enter – no choice. He pushed the door open slowly; it wasn't locked, and the creaking of disuse turned the bishop's veins to ice. It was all he could do to not turn and flee in the dank, putrid air. The sound of wailing felt like a hundred fingernails scraping down a blackboard. It was a precipice at the edge of reason.

The mass of assembled spirits seemed unified to cause, with their voices raised to a crescendo. Their desolation and grief felt to the bishop like the crash of a hammer upon an anvil. Each word seemed to be surrounded in a cauldron of fire and heat.

"My son, they abused my son. You did nothing. You said NOTHING! He took his own life," screamed one voice from the depths of anguish. "It was YOUR fault," was another's wail that surrounded him in a cacophony of pain.

How long the bishop remained in such torment he did not know, because the surrounding darkness had become even more profound. It seemed as if time were a mere figment to a previous epoch. It held no relevance to the currency of his existence. Yet, it was just at that instant he saw the light – a bright, vivid light that pierced the opaque darkness like a laser. Only sensing its origin, he looked up toward the beacon in supplication. It was all he knew how to do. "I'm sorry! I am so sorry for what I have done. But, what of them?" he pleaded, pointing to the sound of desolation. "Will THEY be okay?" he asked to the light.

The glow then enveloped him in a warmth not so far known in this place – wherever he was. "They are loved, eternally. They will see the light, eventually," replied a beautiful voice.

With a flash of light barely discernible, the bishop found himself again surrounded by the mists, although trembling uncontrollably, feeling the suffering coursing through his veins, like heated magma. Then a sound floated errantly through the obscure surrounds. He strained to hear footsteps approaching from a distance, but near, nearing. Yet this mist was like a deep fog over a moonless expanse of sea; he could not discern for love or forgiveness where the sound was coming from. It was precisely then the mists parted.

He had to shield his eyes, for the colour and luminosity of the being's robe was as nothing he had ever seen before. It flowed like the shades of a majestic rainbow, only a hundredfold. The bishop looked down in comparison to the dank greyness of his own attire and wondered how he had ever managed to clothe himself in such drabness to greet one so profound. He wondered why he hadn't noticed before. *Even with all that had happened, you would have thought I'd have noticed how I was attired,* he mused sullenly.

"The colour of our robes is determined within the mists," said the being-of-light in response to the bishop's tacit thoughts. "It is a portent to the path you will soon follow."

Given this brief opportunity to collect himself, the bishop observed his robe as it flowed around his body. From neck to toe it flowed as a cascade, where a point of comparison to earthly garb failed to describe the eminent weave of the fabric. It was as if it were made of light yet woven strongly so that no manner of force could rend its design. It seemed to be a part of him. In life the bishop had previously heard about a person's aura yet had cast off the topic as if it were a construct of the devil. His spirit-being companion, he noticed, had a robe of similar design, but to him, the variance in colours was likened of chalk to cheese – despite the similarity of their stature. What even stood further as a point of difference was his eyes. They sparkled with divinity. His every glance proclaimed and sang to the angels.

"But I don't understand," mumbled the bishop.

"You will, soon," replied the spirit-angel with surety. "First, you must traverse the path that is uniquely yours – no other may intercede." He spoke thus as he pointed fixedly towards a doorway that appeared suddenly out of the mists. Even from a distance, the sense of foreboding emanating from behind the dark portal was tangible in its maleficence. The bishop turned towards the aperture with eyes filled with dread.

"Have mercy, please, I beg you," he stammered, as his face reflected his pending fall from grace. "I am a man of God. All my life was in supplication to His word. I have been a guide to His flock and seen many sinners to His door in redemption. Why? Why must I go? This is a portal to hell I am certain of it."

The angel-being looked at the bishop with a depth of love and compassion. It was a look that cast doubt upon the bishop's resemblance to his previous lifetime.

"Mercy is not the necessity of your redemption, Bishop. Rather, it is our Father's purity of judgement that awaits you behind this portal. All beings, without exception, must enter." The being-of-light paused, with a look that bespoke of the depth of its empathy. "Yet, I know that fear weighs heavy on your heart. Know therefore that the judgement that awaits you is neither eternal nor vindictive, rather, it is probationary and remedial. This is the manifest love and compassion of our Father."

With these last words, the spirit-being faded back into the mists, leaving only the portal, the bishop, and his fear in its wake. The bishop's feet seemed to move forward with volition of their own; every other atom of his being told him to flee. "This is not justice properly served," he screamed into the ethers. Yet he could not stop. His hand reached forward and pushed hesitantly upon the door, which slid open silently with little effort. The overwhelming smell, like burning sulphur, or rancid flesh, assaulted him like a tidal wave. It was all he could do not to turn and plead the angel spirit, once again, for the redemption of mercy. Yet, he could do nothing but move forward into the gloom.

As he trudged forward, a blinding light flashed like a

thousand light bulbs. Behind the light followed a hallowed being. A figure like nothing the bishop could ever have imagined in his wildest imaginings of heaven. It was the most beautiful idol he had ever seen. He fell to his knees in supplication.

"Oh, my God," he cried, as tears of joy filled his eyes. "I knew it would be so! It is all that I had hoped and prayed for! All this time I was in fear, yet the lord of Hosts has heard my prayers." The spirit-angel merely spread its wings of pure white as a gentle sigh fell from the divinity of its mouth. "What is your name so I may address you with proper respect?" stammered the bishop in awe.

"I am called the Archangel Urial. It is my task to see you to proper reward for the actions of the life you have lived."

The bishop's radiant smile described how the weight of his previous fear was now removed from his proper concerns. Rising from his knees, he stood with arms open in blessing and greeting to this being-of-light, the experience of which was beyond his wildest expectations and knowledge of the divine.

"Archangel Urial, by the grace of God, I am most pleased to make your acquaintance," said the bishop, as he felt his voice return to a semblance of its previous authority. "And when do we leave such purgatory to travel to the heavens to sit beside the majesty of our Father?" he asked solemnly.

The archangel merely smiled and slowly cast the expanse of its wings around the bishop's trembling but expectant form. Then, as if by some divine intervention, what was once before the colour of pure white and the sense of abject peace and serenity, the angel's form abruptly transformed. What was before purity, now turned to a burning ember. What was before a gentle gaze from benevolent eyes was now a piercing red glare from the flaming pits of hells-gate. The bishop could not budge from Urial's suffocating embrace. He could only scream in horror.

"For the love of God, who are you? What have I done to deserve such torment? You are not a true being of heaven. You are the devil himself. What is your real name? Tell me. In the name of God, I command you. Let me go, in the name of all that is holy."

The archangel-demon did not relinquish its vice-like clasp upon the bishop's prone form. Only a faint smile passed across its distorted visage.

"My name, dear Bishop, conforms to the evidence of your life."

"What? Speak plainly, you vile creature, that I may understand the nature of your inquiry. In the sight of God, I would see you cast upon the rocks of despair from whence you have come." As if by command, the archangel-demon unfolded its wings to allow the bishop to squirm away from its decrepit embrace. Then, with a flash of light, what was before a hideous demon was, once again, an angelic being of grand majesty. The bishop could only stare in awe at the transformation.

"My name, dear Bishop, speaks to you like an anagram of your eternal soul... Uliar."

A cold sweat trickled down his back as he felt the weight of the archangel's declaration creep through his eternal soul like a miasma. Without control, his legs started to buckle. From the corner of his mouth fell spittle that he could only wipe with his sleeve.

"But, but, I am..."

"You, Bishop, have been a fraud," thundered the archangel. "You have lived your life in a fog of hubris and self-righteous indignation. You have treated your fellow brethren and children with scorn to their well-being, seeking only your elevation in the eyes of God."

The bishop's mouth opened instantly agape yet returned momentarily to righteous indignation and inspired self-assurance.

"And yet I brought many sinners to His door. Many received absolution from my hands in confession so that they may enter Heaven unburdened by sin. I have counted many in the thousands as such."

The archangel's expression softened slightly to declare the bishop's lack of understanding of the natural laws of heaven and earth.

"And why do you think God needs your help to save His children, Bishop? God's love is endless, unbound by each soul's creed or profession. Every soul is a teardrop from His eyes. His love is eternal for all. He is the alpha and the omega. All will come to Him to be renewed. It is what you cause to affect in your fellowman that so declares our Father's judgement. He needed not your intervention to make it so."

Moments passed heavily, but slowly, ever so slowly, did the dawning of divine-understanding shine upon the bishop's limited knowledge of the laws of heaven and earth.

"But how, how can I now atone for such transgressions? How am I to be redeemed in the eyes of God? My earthbound life has passed," he pleaded in fervent desire. The archangel turned slowly to point towards a meandering pathway that appeared silently from the ethers. It descended deep into an expanse that the bishop could not fathom. Although, he did notice that the pathway was of similar colour to the drabness of his attire.

"Go!" commanded the archangel. "Follow this pathway to its destination. There you will see a young man. You will find him much in need of respite from the pain and suffering of abuse under the eyes of your See. He has ears in need of the soothing elixir of the grace of God. Shine divine light into his eyes. Augment his happiness with the comfort of atonement. This, Bishop, is the pathway to your salvation."

With these words uttered, the archangel faded back into the mists. The bishop could only turn slowly toward the designated pathway. But as he took the first step toward his destination, he turned and spoke into the fading mists.

"How long must I administer such truth towards this young

man before redemption blesses my soul?" he inquired.

From the mists came a rumble, like thunder upon the clouds. Then a glorious voice spoke. "Eternity is a long time, my son. Eternity is a long time."

Chapter Two

The Redemption

Wail, bemoan thy fate if thou must,
One's soul be-dammed by deeds of thine own hand.
Look thou to the eyes of the bereft to find redemption within,
On thy knees.

Scales to balance – nay, no clothes shall thee wear,
Be thou judged by thine own hand.
Child of the divine art thou,
Yet untethered from the truth that sets you free.

Born to eternity thou art,
Yet, covered by clouds that ill behove your glory.
Seek not salvation in the stones of the past,
Find glory in the passing of shadows – forgiveness lights.

Know ye not where you stand, dear one?
With me, by my hand.
I love thee more than I can express,
Deny me not, that which I AM, as you are.

The path wasn't hard to follow, the mists had faded slightly,
and the pathway's distinctive colour made it stand out from
the barren wasteland of its origin. It matched the drabness of
his attire – a dull grey, tinged with the odd flash of blue and
yellow streaks. He noticed more how the mouse-hued robe he
wore seemed to envelop him like a blanket. It was as if a tailor
had made it fit the exacting contours of his current form. He
didn't notice any seams or buttons, only that from collar to
toe it flowed over and down his ethereal form like a streaming

robe. Try as he might with exerted effort, he was still unable to take it off. It was as if the garment was him, and he was the garment.

Distracted as he was from watching his robe crimp, sway and flash with the odd errant colour, his feet kept promoting him along the pathway almost of their own volition. He wasn't sure how far he had traversed, and what he certainly failed to notice was the gradual descent. It wasn't so much a sudden jump to an abyss, rather, a more subtle deterioration and meander from the parallel. As he raised his eyes from watching the interplay of streaking lights across the front of his garment, he then became aware of how the colours seemed to change with the movement and passing of his thoughts. Those final words he had heard uttered through the ethers filled his being with dread. "Eternity is a long time, my son." They were words that pierced his heart and throbbed behind his eyes. It was as if the words had been etched into his soul with a heated blade. Am I to trudge this decrepit path forever? he mused as the pathway continued to meander and his feet could only follow command. He watched curiously as this fear-laced thought sent another streak of yellow coursing across the front of his robe about where his heart used to be.

"One's evolution in heaven is never-ending," came a sudden retort like a thunderclap from somewhere out of the ethers. "At least until your atonement is complete."

Looking abjectly towards the voice, the bishop's frown betrayed the complexity of his thoughts. He still couldn't reconcile the conundrum. After all, he had done so many good works in his life. Works that would demand recompense of eternal salvation in the eyes of God.

"What about all the good I did?" he yelled in frustration into the surrounding mists that rolled across his pathway of descent. Only this time he heard just profound silence in response to his inquiry.

He trudged forward through what was a mundane featureless landscape of nothingness. By chance, as he looked askance, he noticed a lone, small blossoming flower by the side of the road. The budding bloom appeared to radiate a divine essence against its background of colourless hue. It seemed the colours of the seven rainbows had been sewn into the delicate petals like a work of art. Even the beautiful scent tickled his senses with a fragrance not before known. Unable to resist, he reached down and touched the petals that reminded him of the softest silk. Looking again at the drabness of his attire and without further prompting, he plucked the flower from its source and sought to place it securely in the lapel of his robe, just to lighten its drabness. Yet, as he placed the flower upon his robe, it crumbled as if it never was. The loveliness of its essence succumbed to dust. The bishop's distress flowed over him like a wave, as he could only stare forlornly at the lost loveliness that now lay scattered upon the dust of the pathway.

"All of my children have the essence of this flower," spoke, once again, the thundering voice from the ethers. "Each child born is a teardrop from my eye. Every child is sprinkled with the divinity of innocence delivered from My hand. When that innocence is stolen, you render the heart of God asunder."

Staring at what remained of the flower, the bishop could only fall to his knees and fumble through the dust on the pathway for what remained of the innocence he had plucked from the eye of God.

"Do you now understand why you are on this pathway?" asked the booming voice.

The drabness of my surroundings was a testament to my inner thoughts. I couldn't shake the desolation from my bones. I felt tired, so very tired. The view from the dirt-encrusted window of my decrepit abode didn't inspire any additional confidence in my outlook. All I saw was devastation. Ruined buildings, crumbled edifices and cratered roads leading to the entranceway of the house I now tried to call home. The problem was, I didn't know how to get out. I knew deep in my soul that this wasn't final, but how I traversed the divide between this place and my potential was far beyond my current capacity.

I looked around the room that had become my castle in search of inspiration, but everything was as drab as my thoughts. Faded colours, encrusted dust and only cobwebs ruled. I couldn't even find any old photographs or pictures to hang a consoling recollection upon. I tried to hold fast to a forgiving memory of my mother, but each time I sought something remotely positive, I was overwhelmed by my sense of shame and disgust at her domineering abusiveness. Not to mention the overriding sense of narcissism that had pervaded her every motive. I wondered at times why she had even bothered trying to be a mother. Somehow the shoe didn't seem to fit. After all, one required a liberal amount of empathy and understanding to be a mum. Qualities of such being completely absent from the person I had called mother.

It kind of made sense to me why my father had shot through when I was so young. The constant barrage of abuse and frayed nerve ends would have been enough to send any sensible person to anywhere else but there. In many ways, I remembered thinking that it was a blessing when she sent me to that boarding school when I was only eleven. The problem was, what had initially been seen as a blessing, turned out to be a bleeding nightmare.

Trying my best not to descend into the vividness of those memories was hard, really hard. The evidence remained. The scars from the lashes on my calves and buttocks were a constant reminder of the years of abuse at the hands of that priest. Then there was the other stuff.

I felt my face crinkle in deference to the still graphic memories of being brutalised by that beast. That so-called 'man of God'.

The pain, aghhh, the pain. It was real at the time, and it was still real now, raw-real – even in this place. And it wasn't just once either. It seemed, because I was the quiet one of the many other young, impressionable boys, I was an easy mark. And the thought that the bastard got away with what he did still burned a hole in my guts.

I sometimes wondered who else knew. I'd tried telling my mother, but she wouldn't listen. She never listened. All she ever kept telling me was that I needed a good education. Then there were those others who sometimes visited the school. One of them was even a bishop if I remembered rightly. He always seemed to have this sanctimonious smile on his face. It wasn't a friendly smile, mind. It was more like an "I'm better than you" or "I know God and you don't" kind of look. Anyway, he seemed pretty friendly with 'the beast', so that was enough reason not to like him.

I remembered one day how 'the beast' and the bishop had come up to me in the vestibule and said, "And this one is favoured by God," as the beast patted my head in a sign of ownership. I remember the bishop looking at me with that inane smile of his and saying, "Blessed are the lambs of God for they shall inherit the earth." I tried to tell him with my eyes that 'the beast' was the devil, but he didn't seem to notice the tears running down my cheeks that I couldn't hold back. Then they entered his office and slammed the door.

It's no good! I HAVE to stop. I can't keep thinking this way. I know it doesn't do me any good, but I can't help it, I thought as I looked around for something, anything to distract me from my torment. But there was nothing, nothing that would help. Even that vague light that often appeared at the top corner of the room didn't help. I'd seen it before. Sometimes it was brighter than others, but this time it was just a dull glimmer of its otherwise potential. Sometimes I could even hear the faint strains of some beautiful music, like choral singers chanting in unison. I could hear it, but then again, I couldn't. It was as if it were reaching for me through a thick fog. It was near, but it was far. I tried reaching out for it once or twice, but I'd given up in resignation when the old pain came back. It just didn't seem right to touch something so beautiful with hands that were so shamefully soiled. I'd even tried praying once or twice, but all that did was regurgitate the old memories of when I attended mass. 'The beast' used to stand behind me with a beatific smile on his face and his erect penis probing through his vestments into my back.

Ah, what the hell, it couldn't get any worse, as I fell to the floor clutching my chest and a puff of dust rose in deference to my knees. But it was then I heard the front gate creak open.

From a distance, the house looked like a remnant from a blitzkrieg, but the pathway led straight to the front gate. Just to make sure, before pushing the rusted bolts aside, he looked around to see if there was somewhere else he would rather be. He even mumbled to himself, "What is this place?" The only response was a deafening silence, but he couldn't stop his hand trembling as he pushed the rusted gate open. Then, instantly, just as he took his first steps towards the house, a fierce wall of flames shot up from seemingly nowhere to bar his way forward to the front portal.

"Holy God," gasped the bishop involuntarily. "I guess whoever lives in this place doesn't want me to be here."

Decisively so, he turned around to retrace his steps back through the gate.

"You will never be saved if you turn around now," resounded the thunderous voice from the ethers. "You too will be lost, eternally."

The bishop looked up from where he thought the voice had come from. "But whoever is inside does not want me to be here," he avowed with a heart full of certainty. "Anyway, if I try to get through those flames I'll be burnt to a cinder."

"You, of all people, should have faith," came the rumbling reply.

Despite the tumultuous ringing in his ears from the pounding in his chest, the bishop entered through the gate and approached the still flaming wall. The heat made his veins run to ice and he had to clasp his ears from the roaring wall of sound that surrounded him in a cacophony of fear. *God help me, God help me,* kept pounding like drumbeats in his ears, as he inched towards the wall with arm outstretched and eyes closed. The closer he got, the more intense the flame, the greater the roar. But then he touched it and almost reeled in horror. It was cold, so very cold. Only his eyes betrayed his awe as he pushed his hand; then his arm; then his whole being through the wall of flames through to the other side.

Stupefied as he was, it was then he saw the silhouette. A man, standing behind the dirt-encrusted and firmly closed window. But he saw him. He was there, all right. At that very same instant, a flash of memory of a small boy streaked across his mind, but it was so fleeting, it was impossible to hold to it.

By some force of inspiration, he looked down at his vestment. It was as if it were alive. There were sparks of yellow, blue and red flickering like an errant sparkler as his heart pounded with the sound of thunder behind his eyes. Yet, he moved forward towards the front door. *I guess this is what faith is,* was the thought that provided some solace to his fear.

The boards on the ruined porch moaned in deference to disuse when he placed his first tentative step upon them. He could hear whoever was inside shuffling about as if they were trying to find another place to be. Then he knocked on the door slowly... once, twice, then a third time.

"Go away. Leave me alone. I know who you are. You're one of them..." cried my voice, taut with overwrought emotion. The bishop could not recognise the voice, though it was at such a pitch he could easily fathom the depths of its torment.

"I, I don't know who you are, or, even why I am here," stammered the bishop as his nose came within millimetres of the still firmly closed front portal. "But I was told to come... by this voice..."

My mouth was welded shut to reply. It was only my effort to fortify my defences that caused the shuffling and banging sounds from inside the house. Then... CRASH. The large projectile I threw almost took his head off as it smashed through the feeble portal.

"I said, LEAVE ME ALONE. You cannot help me," I screamed. "You are the one who put me here..."

Despite his close brush with calamity, the bishop could only stand and stare, mouth agape, through the hole in the door. The power of my words had pierced his soul. It took an eternity of moments for him to find his proper wits.

"What? I, I don't know what you mean..." he managed to mumble.

"BULLSHIT! You knew! You knew all along. You knew what he was doing, but you chose not to see. You chose not to hear... You're a LIAR! You are a fraud!"

The bishop could not stop his knees buckling as he crumpled onto the errant dust on the porch and lay sobbing. He couldn't find any words. All he could find were tears as he felt his chest cleave with the anguish of a thousand cuts. It was as if he was being torn asunder by a force greater than anything he had ever known.

The pain was the only barometer of time in this place – wherever he was. He had no idea how long he stayed prone on the porch smothered in his tears. All he could see was the dust on the porch that had formed a small pool of congealed mud around his tears. His chest felt like it had been severed by a meat-cleaver. Then he heard the door creak open.

I suppose it doesn't matter anyway. What more can he do to me that he hasn't already done, I thought as I poked my head slowly through the ajar door. *I mean, look at him. The poor bastard couldn't do any more harm*, I mused, peeking around the frame as a smile tried to dredge its way up towards my face. But I still couldn't bring myself to go outside. I turned, just leaving the door open a little, and went back to the place on the lounge that I knew so well... and waited. I could barely open my eyes when the door was pushed fully open and the bishop came in.

"Don't come any closer," I shouted as I held the comfort of a soft cushion firmly to my chest. "I don't want you here. Go away! GO AWAY! Please."

"No, I won't. I WON'T," shouted the bishop with equal ferocity. "I don't know why I am here. But, before God, I will not leave. Do you hear me?"

The force of these words seemed to cause us both to freeze like pillars of salt facing Gomorrah. The gelid air between us became alive with some kind of potential that neither could see nor pierce. Seconds ticked to eternity, but it was the bishop who finally broke it open when he looked around my decrepit abode.

"Is this where you live – here? I mean, I'm not exactly sure where we are, but is this your home?"

I couldn't think of anything in reply as I brushed away some errant dust from the corner of the lounge that had been bothering me.

"Do you mind if I sit?" he asked.

I couldn't respond, my voice didn't seem to work, but I rewarded him with a faint shrug and pointed towards an unused and comfortless chair. The thundering sound of silence then filled the space between us again in countless heartbeats – some more painful than others.

The bishop tried valiantly to pull the fleeting memory image of a young boy to heel, but he still couldn't grasp it. Of all the people he had ministered to. All those who had hung on his words for salvation, and there were many, this one just didn't stick. He knew deep down that he had seen this person before, but he just could raise the recall.

"I, I know you know who I am," he started tentatively. "But I'm sorry, I don't know. I just can't remember. What is your name?"

It was as if a tsunami had engulfed the delicate remnants of the man sitting before him – me. The bishop saw my hands cover my mouth, trying to stop my face from collapsing. My eyes betrayed the pain of a thousand lashes. What was worse, the bishop could feel the same pain. It was as if we were one-and-the-same, like kindred spirits in a cataclysm of desolation. The bishop could only wrap his arms around himself and rock backwards and forwards on the flimsy chair to abate the depths of the pain that I too was experiencing. The heartbeats of grief rolled through us for moments of eternity.

But then, without any sense of warning, I jumped from the lounge and quickly traversed the space between us, and I placed a crooked finger to the bishop's forehead. Somehow, I just knew he would be immediately transported to the scene...

The first image was the clearest. At least it held the least pain. He saw himself speaking with a young boy in the company of THAT priest. He remembered saying, "Blessed are the lambs of God for they shall inherit the earth." He remembered seeing tears in the boy's eyes but thought they were because of his blessing. The next images told him how wrong he was. How very wrong. They were a blur of horrid torment. The images of the poor boy being raped and abused by THAT priest were torture to behold. He tried averting his proper senses from the images, but he couldn't. He had to look as they burned into his soul.

"Oh, heavenly Father. What have I done? What did he do to

you?" cried the bishop as he fell to his knees in supplication. Lifting his head and staring through tears, he could only watch, mutely, as my pointed finger turned to a fist trying not to strike him. As I did so, the collar of my robe fell away briefly from my neck. The vivid purple puce of the scar that circled my throat was plain to see. Then my tormented soul could stomach no more.

"Go! Go away. You have seen everything. Now you know. It's too late for me. Your redemption cannot be found here," I screeched through anguish that scraped along the bottom of my burning pit.

The bishop could barely focus outside the pain. The only thing he could hear was the pounding of his heart in his ears. But the thunder was trying to tell him something. He couldn't hear it. He couldn't hear it. Wait! But then he knew...

"I will not! I will not leave you again!" he asserted stoically, rising from his knees. "Not until I am forgiven."

"But don't you see? I cannot forget. The memories are burnt into my soul. The pain is always there. How can I forgive?"

The bishop stood rooted to his spot but reconciled to his purpose. "I, I don't know," he replied tentatively. "But maybe we can ask."

"Ask? Ask who? There is no one else here."

"Yes, there is," said the bishop as he looked up towards the corner of the room towards the vivid light that had suddenly appeared with vibrance. "There. Look!" he said, pointing.

As I looked up towards the light, the bishop could see a spark fleet across my eyes, a vague glimmer that had previously been absent. "But what do we do now?" I asked.

"We pray. We pray, together."

Reaching for the other's hand as we knelt on the floor, we both looked towards the light. Our words then formed a duet of grace as we chanted in unison.

"Our Father who art in heaven,

Hallowed be Thy name,
Thy kingdom come..."

Chapter Three

The Renewal

Unburdened shall thee be, to lighten passage forth,
Yet, 'tis burdens imposed that shall be relieved.
Torment rent by others will not your misfortune be,
Love's chorale sings light caress to return the grace to thee.

Would'st thou know me, do you not see?
Who am I, where do I be?
Be ye blind, or must I help ye see,
Beyond who, or what, you think yourself to be.

Look in awe, see the majesty before thee,
Believe if you will, it matters not.
For that which is truth lies open before ye,
Feel the power within, asleep it lies, till dawn alights.

The angel bears gifts for thee and thine,
Burdens stand nought before the supreme.
I would scarce believe, if seen not to mine eyes,
The grace of the lord cast his light into thee.

"Athar, Athar, come, it is time," were the words we both heard coming from outside as we rose simultaneously, somewhat shakily it must be said, from our knees.

The bishop had only just managed to open his eyes and the pressure of my hand in his own reminded him of security that had been in meagre supply. I looked around at the completely transformed room in a state of inspired awe. What had before been a monument to disuse and devastation was now a renewed work of spirit-in-progress. There was colour and vibrancy. The drab pallor of the crumbled interior had been replaced with a sense of expectation. It appeared as if a décor doctor had reconstructed it with an artistic, loving hand. The bishop's eyes shone with inner glee as he saw the first faint smile crack upon my stunned visage. Then we looked at one another in response to the unexpected and unexplained voice.

"Athar, it is time. Your journey awaits you," came the voice.

To the bishop, the voice felt like a caress of silk to his proper senses. It almost made him swoon.

He looked across to me questioningly. "Who is Athar?"

The shrug from my shoulders was sign enough to deepen the puzzle, but it was I that rose first to open the door to the voice outside.

The light permeated everything it touched as soon as the door was opened. It seemed to fill every niche and crevice in the room. So much so that we both had to shield our eyes with our hands so our sight could pierce what lay behind the ethereal glow. From the light then emerged the most beautiful seraphim. From the bishop's perspective, it looked like a child, but it was more than that. Nor could I swear to the specifics of its gender, for it appeared neither male nor female, only that it was more than the sum of both. Its radiance of light seemed to come from within. Despite its small stature, divinity, innocence, grace, humility were all qualities that emanated from its every pore.

The bishop could only watch in amazement as I, who was before tormented by the power of bitter memories, now stood transfixed and transforming before this being-of-light. He watched as the child took my hand. He could only stare in wonder at the tears that fell in a cascade down my face. He could only smile in knowing that a once troubled soul had been released to the divine. But a question formed in his mind and creased his brow in the asking.

"Who is Athar?"

The seraphim turned with a radiant smile in response. "Why

this is Athar," it said, holding my hand. "This is his real name. We all have real names in heaven."

The bishop's brow deepened, as he felt a wave of sorrow pierce his breast with remorse. "I didn't even know his name," he mumbled, as the remorse did finally pass and left in its wake a solace of compassion. "But where do you take him?"

The seraphim's childlike eyes brightened with grace as it looked up towards the ethers. "First, he must rest, for his trials have been many. Then, we will take him to the healing arena where his spirit will be renewed."

"Oh!" replied the bishop with a face of limited understanding. "And what then?"

"Only he can know how far the grace of God will take him."

The angel then turned to me as he and I lifted, yes, lifted and soared upwards into the ethers, whence the bishop could see us no more.

Looking up into what now was only azure light and traces of mist, the bishop asked, "Will I ever see him again?"

"Yes, of course," came the resounding rumbled reply from the clouds. "You are kindred spirits. Look!"

As directed, the bishop looked down suddenly. To his astonishment, exiting out from his chest, just near his heart, he watched the silver cord streaming up towards the heavens. I saw his eyes fly open in wonder at what was there but had not before been noticed. It was then I saw that same beautiful cord attached fixedly to my own heart.

"What is that?" I could not help but ask my guardian.

"Love links soul with soul and has the power to bridge any gulf if it is only strong and true," replied the seraphim.

The bishop didn't bother to close the gate as he left. It seemed rather pointless. Even as he made his way from the grounds, he could only gasp in witness at the house's slow crumble into dust. Within but a few heartbeats, what was before the construct of rocks and stone, was now but a figment of the imagination. He couldn't help but stare as the final cornerstone of the house dissolved as if it never had been. He turned to leave, not knowing to where or what, yet something made him pause momentarily. Perhaps it was the silent voice he thought he heard within. "Don't go. Wait. Watch!" said the voice, in response to which he could only stare.

From out of the ruin, forcing itself through the dust and debris came a small crocus. It pushed its way up through the surface with undeniable determination. First, there was one, then came another. Then three, then too many to count. So many buds unfurled and blossomed to caress their dawning celebration.

"It's the same! It's the same colour," exclaimed the bishop in awe, as he inhaled deeply with conscious awareness of the divine at play. With delight, he noticed it was the same bloom he had inadvertently plucked before – only multiplied by a factor of many. He swooned in delight at the welcomed assault tickling his senses. Then, looking up to the ethers that swirled gently above him, "Is it okay? Can I?" he asked.

"Of course," came the distant but adjacent reply from the ethers.

He bent down slowly to gently touch one of the delicate petals. "Thank you," he intoned when removing the flower from its source and placing it in his lapel. A vague shadow of recollection passed across his face as he prayed the same result of destruction would not ensue. He smiled and sighed deeply when it did not. His nose twitched with delight as he sniffed the delicate bloom, then turned to resume his travels on the pathway.

Smiling as he did, at the flower's distraction, he had not noticed to what he now bore astonished witness. "Oh, my God, the pathway." It was not at all the same as the one that directed him to this place. It too had transformed. What was before a drabness of greying dirt and desolate barren, was now a field of flowers and rolling green beyond his most vivid imaginings. He couldn't help but smile. A similar change had occurred in his attire. It too seemed to mirror the quality of its surroundings. His robe that was before dull and drab, was now also a vestment in renewal.

His brow furrowed at how this transformation was possible. But the questions were starting to queue up in his mind. He certainly knew that he wasn't alone. Not in this place – wherever he was. But given the limitations of his understanding, he figured perhaps patience was the better resolution to his present dilemmas. Somewhere within the central crucible of his being was the sense that all would be presently revealed. Somehow, he managed to remain passively content and just walk and watch the environs as they seemed to deepen with grace – he a mere thankful observer to the offering.

I heard the bells pealing even before my eyes laid witness to the giant edifice I was approaching. I turned to look quizzically at the beautiful angel-child who was still holding my hand.

"Yes, this is our destination," said he in answer to my tacit question. "The bells summon the many souls to the calling. Look..." it said, pointing towards the large arena-like structure that loomed like a colossus out of the mists. I could only stare as I watched a plethora of so many beautiful souls advancing through the giant colonnades that held the magnificent structure aloft. The reflections from their many and various-coloured robes were as nothing previously witnessed by this uninitiated observer. For my newly opened eyes, it appeared like a thousand rainbows had formed a sea of ever-rippling hue.

The angel smiled at the expressed wonder of his charge.

"Come," it said, "your renewal awaits," as I felt the pressure of my guardian's hand increase ever so slightly and urge me towards our destination.

I was almost too overwhelmed to count the many radiant beings as I gaped in awe at the crowd in attendance at the gathering. Our entrance through the large portals seemed to be in exact timing with other beings-of-light and their accompanying wards. My ears pricked at what was before me – a clamour of a thousand-voice chorale in unison as they entered the stadium. To me, it sounded much like the sound of "Ohmmm" being chanted. Being a sound foreign to my ears, my hand tensed ever so slightly, but my guardian angel only smiled in reassurance. "Fear not," it said with an expression that described divinity. "They are here for you. This is your time of renewal."

The chanting felt like a salve over my frayed edges. I could only obediently follow as my guardian directed me to one of the many reclining beds in the centre of the arena. I was beckoned to lie on the couch, noticing the other weary souls – some severely disabled, it must be said – being directed to do the same on their respective recliners. The last thing I remembered was that the lounge seemed to envelop my form like a well-worn comforter. It felt custom fit for my purpose alone. I couldn't help but close my eyes as the soft resonance of the chanting then washed over me like a gentle brook over jagged rocks. Then the lights went out. Or, more specifically, my lights went out.

As the bishop crested a slight rise, he espied at a near distance a rather large oak tree. At some distance, it didn't appear particularly unusual, nor out of place in its context. But there was something about the way the branches fanned out and spread its leaves. Like a boon to all wayfaring travellers. He approached, hearing a soft cadence of beautiful music or chanting. It seemed to emanate from the tree itself, but this was too much for his practical and uninitiated synapses to digest. He was even struggling to remain content to approach and allow the music to fill the crevices of his being.

Maybe it was a trick of the light, or perhaps his proper senses were not attuned to the many and varied hues of the landscape. But when the man appeared, he could have sworn he had exited from within the tree itself. The bishop jumped with a start when the being spoke.

"I've been waiting for you," said the man as he brushed an errant leaf from his robe.

The bishop noticed immediately how the man's robes seemed to shimmer with a depth of green hue that he could barely describe with words. It was as if each colour was as deep as a forest. Each sparkle appeared to denote a minim of wisdom or grace. Then there was something else. Something that was there but he couldn't quite grasp. Like a thought that flew by too quickly to read, or a memory of something full of meaning, but hard to remember.

"I, I know you, don't I?" stammered the bishop as he came to stand before this new elemental.

"Does the shepherd not recognise his sheep?" he replied somewhat cryptically, as he motioned with his hands to come and place weighted concerns in recline against the huge trunk. With backs secure against the strength of the oak, they both reposed in ease and allowed the silence of the quiet chant to fill the space between them and serve as an elixir to their communal spirit.

It could have been the divine essence emanating from the tree that caused his lapse from conscious awareness, but the bishop found it impossible to hold fast to his alert senses. His head drooped forward to what was sleep that could not be denied. He seemed to drift into a dreamscape where everything was real, but nothing could be touched. He could feel, he could sense, but he could not alter. Of the many images that floated by and he could not hold on to, there seemed just one that held the recurrence of a theme. It was as if his previous life was held in thrall to what had previously been denied or repressed.

He shook his head and creased his brow to adjust to the complexity of what he was trying to see in the gloom. The dark room in which he was enclosed seemed to move with the malevolence of shadows, yet there were no doors, nor apertures to allow any light he could fathom. Fear rose like a cresting wave in his chest as he felt the darkness like a spectre pecking at his eyes, willing them to be opened.

"What is this place? Where am I? Please help me," he yelled, fitfully trying to feel his way around his entrapment without the possibility of success. Only the depth of silence and the sound of his heavy breathing filled his ears.

"LET ME GO. Leave me be, whoever you are," he yelled, as much to repress the terror that welled in his breast. "I AM THE BISHOP. I do not deserve such torment."

A sound, like screaming, softly at first, then with ever-increasing intensity pierced the gloom like a sword heated within a fiery cauldron. It was a sound that pierced the silence like the shriek of a hundred discordant violins. At first, he reasoned that it was perhaps only his mind playing fearfully with torments long repressed, but it could not be. The sound had so much resonance. It was alive and replete with malice.

Not knowing what else to do, he crunched himself into a ball in the corner of the darkness and clasped his hands to his ears. It seemed like the only respite to the constancy of the ever-deepening sound that would not sway from its terror. It refused to yield to his protestations.

"I am the Bishop! By the power of God, I command you to be gone," he ordered. But the orders were void. This dark night of the soul torment seemed to persist for an eternity in a time that did not identify itself in anything but the present moment. He could only feel the wetness of tears tumbling down his cheeks, but they didn't shine any light upon the profundity of the darkness.

Time ticked to eternity and seemed to last like an ever-long heartbeat, but then, just as suddenly as it had started, the dreadful sound ceased, and a silent chant seemed to pierce the edges of his despair.

"Who are you?" were the words that echoed around the confines of his entrapment. But speaking in reply only made the words resonate in echo as they played ping-pong around the walls.

"Why am I here," he screamed fitfully into the darkness. "God, why have you abandoned me? Why do you cast these stones upon me, your servant?"

Then, from out of the depths of the darkness appeared a light, a bright shimmering, pinpoint light that held him transfixed.

"I have never abandoned you. I love you more than you will ever know," replied a beautiful voice from the depths of everywhere. "But you cannot escape the consequences of your deeds. Forgiveness is at the heart of your ultimate realisation. It is the cleansing of your soul."

The bishop could scarcely contain the anger that erupted like a volcano within his breast.

"Forgiveness. Forgiveness for what? I was Your bishop. The leader of Your flock. Guardian for a multitude of souls," he roared as he gasped to capture a breath and wipe the sweat leaking into his eyes. "Why do you treat me thus?" The bishop's heavy gasps were just a prelude to a further outpouring. "Sure, I made mistakes. What leader of men would not? Weigh me to balance to see the scales tipped firmly in favour of Thy flock."

"My son, he that is greatest among you, shall be a servant to all.

A man is not judged by the virtue of creed or profession. Nor the power vested by title. In heaven, the emperor wears no clothes. Sanctity resides in the mercy that you practised, not what you preached. Your role as Bishop was to serve and protect my children, never to defend the bastions of the church."

As suddenly as a flashing light arched across his eyes and the voice abated, he awakened with a start to the familiarity of his previous surrounds. The scrape of the tree's bark felt comforting on his back as he turned to see the man sitting peacefully in contemplation of a divinity that only he was able to witness. Nothing seemed to have changed. Time had not seemingly moved, yet many things felt different. He shook his head to clear the webs of confusion.

"But, but I, I just heard these words. I was in this cell..."

"Yes, yes, I know," he replied as he rose from his seat with a deep sigh. "We have all been there..."

"But where? Where was I?"

"It is called the dark night of the soul. It is where you must confront who you really are, not who you think you are."

The bishop's forehead creased so fully his brows almost fought for the open space between his eyes.

"So, I am not who I think I am? But, if you've been waiting for me, surely you know who I am."

"My job is not to tell you what to know, it is to show you how to see."

"But who are you?" the bishop asked hesitantly, still in need of clarification to the complexities.

"My name is Elijah," was the only offering to the inquiry before lapsing again into silence. Then, just as suddenly as he had spoken, Elijah pointed in the direction of their intended travel.

"Come. We must go. It is time. Your lessons await."

The bishop could do nothing but rise and brush the fallen leaves errantly from the front of his robe.

"Go? Go where? Lessons? What lessons?"

Elijah ignored each of these questions and just started to walk briskly towards the intention of his destination. The bishop had to hasten his steps to remain in touch.

He was certain that he still didn't know much of how things worked in this place, but he was beginning to grasp that nothing happened by chance. All things seemed to be divinely inspired, even memories of his previous life. It was then that a face flashed across his rather full banks of memory. It was a face he knew. He even remembered the time and place. It made him halt suddenly in his tracks.

"I, I know you, don't I, Elijah?"

The man, without turning, just stopped, but even so, it was easy to see the quaint smile that formed wrinkles around the wisdom of his eyes.

"You are the... You were at the hospice," he stammered.

"Yes, I am. I was there."

"You! At the hospice our church had established to help the poor and dying! You were there a long time. We used to call you the 'Gatekeeper', didn't we? You used to bathe and cleanse them when they had soiled. Held their hands when they were afraid. Comfort them as they passed."

Elijah could only nod in confirmation.

"You used to help those who were dying, didn't you? I remember now. You once told me that it was your job to open the door so that each soul could walk through without fear. You said that, didn't you?"

Elijah just nodded again but then started to proceed with haste towards the destination unknown.

"But why were you here to meet me? Where are you taking me, now? I was the bishop. It was my hospice. In my See, after all," he asked somewhat belligerently as he caught up.

Just then, just as they crested a slight rise, their destination became self-evident. It could not be missed, and its view seemed to melt all questions into dust. From afar it seemed rather like a large colosseum and the bishop could only stare in wonder at the magnificence of the edifice. Elijah could only shape his hands in prayer and whisper his gratitude, before turning to the bishop.

"Come," he said as his feet, once again, started with intent towards their purpose. "It is time for you to see the magnificence of our heavenly Father's work. How His grace and love give rise to eternity for all."

"But how... why me?" asked the bishop with eyes that betrayed his lack of understanding of heaven, earth and his place within.

"Because, my friend, you have a grand role to fulfil... if you so choose."

Given his guide's haste, the bishop only caught up when Elijah reached for his hand as they were about to pass through the shimmering iron gates between the great colonnades.

"Come. We are in retard. It is about to begin."

The bishop didn't seem to mind Elijah's reticence with the spoken word. He figured it might be something to do with his experiencing rather than the telling. Anyway, what unfolded before his eyes took much of his breath away and focused his thoughts to the pinpoint of the moment. Manoeuvring with a smile between welcoming souls, Elijah found their two vacant seats next to the aisle. Sitting down, he felt the chanting of the crowd lift his soul to another stratosphere. It was like being in an express elevator to the summit of a mountain. It felt as if he was being cleansed from the inside out. He glanced to notice that even Elijah had joined the choral choir of chanting. Then, as the chanting peaked to a crescendo, he could only stare agog at what unfolded before his scarcely believing gaze.

Late as they were being seated, the bishop noticed many lounge beds in the centre of the arena already occupied by sleeping forms. Unfamiliar as it all was, it appeared as if the beds themselves had been custom fit to each occupant. To the bishop, it looked as if each repose had been moulded to the form of its charge. Transfixed as he was, distraction came when two others approached through one of the many portal gates. One soul, heavily disabled, was unable to walk unassisted. She was handled with great care by what could only be described as a guardian angel – not unlike the seraphim to whom he had previously borne witness.

Despite this seraphim's childlike stature, the radiance that emanated from its divine countenance completely overwhelmed any other perception of fragility. With the greatest of care, the guardian-angel helped its charge onto the lounge, whereby the lounge shaped to take command of the poor soul's care and comfort.

Another soul and its guardian soon followed, this one suffering under the weight of a great malady. His body was but a skeletal form of what had been a robust man, the ravages from his previous life that had taken such a devastating toll. Disease had rendered this once-mighty form to something barely recognisable to its original incarnation. But, as before, the wretched man's guardian was able to lead its charge to the awaiting lounge with great care.

Only with great difficulty could the bishop avert his glance and turn to Elijah. He so wanted to ask the purpose of what he was witnessing, but Elijah was chanting. The majestic look on the gatekeeper's face called a sudden halt to any pending inquiry. Anyway, what happened next made all the bishop's questions dissolve into unimportance. The crowd's unified chanting abruptly faded when all the central lounges had been occupied. Even to the bishop's untrained receptors, the final "Ohmmm" rolled over the vast assembly like a gentle swan of serenity.

Then, from seemingly nowhere, a divine Being stepped forth into the middle of the arena. Tall, calm, and majestic best described the Being's stature, but being branded by definition or form would only cause injury to the language that attempted such ineptitude. Rather, a sound refuge and shelter of God-like compassion more portrayed the grander sum of the totality of these best parts. The Being's robe radiated with what could only be pronounced by the glow of the sun, with streaks of green that flashed like lightning from within the folds, as if the colour was the essence of its purpose.

The angel-being then lifted his hands to the sky in a summons, starting to chant in a voice of the divine, softly at first, then much louder. It sounded to the bishop like slow-rolling thunder. Then, as if by some divine magic, a ball of light appeared between his raised hands. Rolling his hands, as if kneading soft dough, sparks of energy formed into a ball of energy of augmenting power. Sparks flew like lightning from within the centre of the spinning magnetic ball. Then, when it was the moment known only to himself, the angel directed laser-like beams of light toward and into each of the occupants on the recliners.

The bishop's eyes stood awed in wonder as he witnessed the light enter and surround each of its subjects, to caress each one in a soft glow of immense power. Time seemed to bear no reference to the relevant as he watched all this magnificence unfold. Yet, it didn't seem to matter. The only thing that concerned was what happened when the angel folded his hands. The glow of the magnetic laser lights faded back into the magnetic ball. A soft sigh seemed to emanate as one from the multitude of the assembled. The sigh sounded like a communal expression of gratitude as the light returned to the grace of its source.

With the power of the magnetic having now been properly dispensed, the angel merely smiled gracefully and walked quietly from the arena. The bishop felt fit to bursting. He could feel his heart pounding with a thousand drums as he could not stop staring towards what now unfolded.

Upon their awakening, each lounge seemed to release its gentle hold over its occupant. He gasped as each soul, without exception, gaped in awe at their surroundings as they opened their eyes. He could only stare in amazement when observing that each person, before sick or disabled, was now hale and hearty. They had been renewed. They had been cured. Their previous body of malady had returned to one of strength and vitality. By the grace of God, they had been transformed. Straining to take his eyes from the unfolding events, the bishop could barely gasp for air. There were so many questions stuck in his throat, he could hardly turn to his friend, Elijah, to form proper words.

Luckily Elijah came to succour. "By the grace of our Father, souls are released from the burdens of illness, deformity or disability of spirit imposed by others into their eternal life in heaven. The burdens are relieved," explained Elijah before he once again started to chant.

But what then took place spun all else before it into a vortex. The bishop could only stare, mouth open in amazement, as Athar rose from one of the lounges. He was radiant.

Chapter Four

The Unfolding

Let there be light, sayeth He of most high,
And thus, all things in heaven and earth came to be.
Why then doth mine eyes abide so much horror?
Woe-betide thy temptations which bind – lust, envy, greed,
  wrath.

If thou could see what I have seen, sin you would not,
Cast aside you would those temptations of impermanent
  flesh.
Eternities bind to such folly!
Escape from its clutches, I beseech thee.

Yet, our host's hands stand ever-open, never absent His
  pledge.
I have given thee light, open your eyes.
Take my hand within thine,
Fear not.

But what now? Why me?
But a drop in an ocean am I.
You are sacred – my teardrop, said He,
Lead thou me on, said I.

The bishop didn't know whether to cry for joy or sing in praise.
The extraordinary nature of what he had just witnessed in the
stadium was enough to fill the coffers of his everlasting memory
banks for eternity. To bear witness to the grace of renewal for
each of the poor souls under care was a journey to the majesty
of the true nature of God. Then, to see Athar in full glory, now

resplendent in a robe of majestic hues, was like a salve to a still-open wound. He could do little else but stand mute as a statue, unable or unwilling to move lest something else occur to excel that which already had befallen.

For his part, Elijah had finished chanting and was quietly watching his friend process the enormity of the many moments.

"Come, there is more to be done," Elijah exclaimed in his comforting staccato style. At least it helped to break through the self-imposed stupor into which he had fallen. Elijah's hand gave more comfort as they moved solemnly back through the portal gates. Although scarcely alert to his surroundings, he could at least hear the myriad of voices raised on high by the departing assembly in proclamation to the grace of God. It was all so much for the bishop to process.

"Where do we go now?" he inquired with a voice that seemed barely capable of proper function – as if in need to be oiled before next use.

A twinkle passed across Elijah's eyes as he glanced at his friend.

"You have seen but a glimpse of the majesty of heaven at work," he said with his half-smile. "Now you need to see the other parts."

"What other parts? Is there more?"

Elijah inhaled deeply before seeking words that best described what was next to come. "I'm not sure if you're going to like this part," he explained as he set forth along one more pathway towards another of his intended destinations of discovery. The bishop had to hasten to catch up, again.

I instantly recognised the love that emanated from my new surroundings. To compare my current vista with the pallor of my previous settings was to compare sunlight to darkness. I stood entranced as I looked out from the open window of the house that I now called my own in heaven. What I felt, breathing deeply, was consecrated life. Everything was alive with abundance. The depth of colour of the many and varied flora in the garden seemed to be a declaration to the word of divinity. Everything was in harmony. Everything had a purpose in symphony with the other, all declaring praise to the lord of heaven and earth.

"God made heaven and earth and all things therein," exclaimed the voice from behind me. I turned, startled, at the sudden break to my contemplation. The dulcet voice belonged to the person, or more rightly the grand spirit that had before directed the proceedings at the arena. His bearing and stature seemed even more magnificent standing now close before me. Yet, the essence of love and compassion that exuded from his every pore could not be mistaken. Even now, so close as he was, I could only begin to perceive the depths of his divinity, but it did not seem to matter. All that seemed to my concern was that he was here.

I stumbled to find a proper voice. All my powers of energy seemed to be drawn into a vortex that was the divine being before me. Yet, words did come, eventually.

"Who, who are you? Why? Why me?" was all I could stammer.

The smile that radiated from him was like looking into the sun. He moved with grace, like silk upon rough, to stand and gaze at the reverence of our outlook. Then he moved gracefully to a seat on the balcony overlooking the garden, inviting me to do the same beside him.

"May I be permitted to answer your last question first, dear Athar?" as I could but stare, open-mouthed.

"You, as you always were, are a divine teardrop from the eye of our Father, both in heaven and earth."

"I am?" I stuttered. "But I have only just thrown off the yoke of my previous transgressions, the burden of my previous life that so weighed me to shackles. How can it be that I am now so blessed in the eyes of God?"

"The weight that each soul bears unto heaven is but the consequence of what they have reaped from their actions, and the actions of others, on earth. 'What you sow, so shall you reap' is an infallible law, both of heaven and earth. All shall be revealed. No thought or action insignificant. All remembered to record. Yet, in heaven, sins imposed by others are not those that need to be borne by the self. It is this law that lays open the pathway of redemption at our feet. This is the law that guides us to realise the divinity that resides ever within ourselves."

My frown was soothed somewhat as I sought inspiration from the beauty of the vista before me, yet the conundrum remained.

"Behold," said this being-of-light as he pointed towards a small crocus just beginning its journey into the wide expanses beyond the previous confines of its interment in the garden. "Do you think the seed of the budding flower knows what it is to become as it grows to break the surface of its previous incarnation? If the budding crocus is smitten by errant hand, is it the fault of the crocus?"

"No, I guess it is not."

"Within each crocus is a power beyond all contemplation – the power to realise itself in its fullest bloom, and to express the wonder that is inherent within the core of its very being. Yet, it knows not its fullest potential, only that it must fulfil the divinity of its purpose. This, my dear Athar, is the grand power given to all sentient beings through the blessed love of our Father. Any effort to stymie the growth of the crocus is a sin that needs to be redeemed by the offending hand."

I could only bow my head before the wisdom that was now plain to my sight.

"All beings are so blessed. There are no exceptions to the laws of heaven and earth."

"Yet, my suffering was great at the hands of the church and

her supposed guardians to the gateway of heaven. I ask again, for God's mercy does not seem so evident, that He allows His children to be so abused by base men divorced from the hand of God's grace."

"Come," he said, as he rose to move towards the garden beyond the confines of my abode. "Oh, and by the way, you may call me by my name. I am known as Atticus."

I was initially too stunned even to move, as he disappeared around a near corner.

"Wow," I said when I managed to catch up. "My grandfather's name was Atticus. I remember him when I was but a child. I loved him very much, but he died when I was young. Yet I remember his love so well."

"Yes, I know," he replied with a faint hint of a knowing smile. "Come over here, I want to show you something." A few paces around a turned corner brought us both to the intended destination.

Atticus had stopped at the base of a large tree. A tree that radiated a sense of magnificence that I had never before encountered. Strength seemed to emanate from the very essence of its tangled roots and expansive trunk. Its many branches each held a plethora of leaves that all sang a divine cadence. The scent from its multitude of flowers held a tint of divine nectar that would satisfy the gods.

"Come, Athar, touch the trunk with me."

Without hesitation, I reached forward and placed my palms upon the bark of the magnificent edifice. Instantly, I started to swoon. My vision blurred as I was transported to somewhere that I could not yet describe:

I was but a mere observer to the injury about to be caused. I could only watch, mutely, as I saw the man take the sharpened axe to the base of the fledgeling tree, much similar, but much smaller to that which I knew in this heavenly dream. With a dozen hefty blows before the axe man's mirthless might and power, the tree could only succumb, toppling to the forest floor with the sound of thunder.

All at once, I removed my hands from the tree as if burned by its touch. I could only stare in deference to the wanton and senseless destruction I had just witnessed.

"But now you see, Athar, that our tree has not perished. It yet thrives in the magnificence of God's benevolence and prospers to give solace and succour to all creatures seeking its shelter and bounty. The sharpness of the axe man's blade did not blunt the life and true purpose of the tree's existence before God. It yet lives and grows stronger."

As my hand caressed the bark, I felt the insight of the tree's history radiating like a beacon within my soul.

"Yes!" I replied with a voice that was beginning to reflect my deeper understanding. "And it is the same with me, is it not?"

Atticus' smile of delight was almost enough, but he added to it with a dulcet voice, "Yes, and so be it for all of God's flowers."

After Atticus had taken his leave, I was at liberty to repose once more on the balcony that was now my own for such contemplation, although his words before departure still resonated like a peal of thunder. "You may repose here for as long as you wish. This is your haven. Yet know that much more awaits in the unfolding before God's grace is complete," he had said.

The air seemed to thicken and cloy in his chest like an errant malignancy. It felt more so the further they traversed upon this descending roadway to only Elijah knew where. It was hard not to notice the similarity between the road that had previously led him to the abode of Athar. But this road was significantly more decrepit.

This pathway reminded a fire of its trail of destruction

through pristine habitat. Charred remains of trees and blackened bush served only to assail its travellers with a sense of despair lingering after calamity. Flora that had once stood vibrant and majestic now bore witness to a trail of devastation. It reminded the bishop of a time on earth when he had witnessed the ravages of a bushfire that had scorched the earth of his See over which he then presided. Only worse, much worse.

The air seemed putrid and filled with the cries of despair. He walked in silence awash with astonishment, as a profound sense of animus gripped at his being. The tightening of his chest made him feel like a drowning man in search of the luxury of air. Sensing his unease, Elijah stopped suddenly and motioned to speak to his charge.

"In heaven there exists torments far worse than your imagination of hell," he said, pointing as a dark, forbidding door appeared suddenly before them. "Yet, you must know, that it is all heaven."

"But if this is heaven, how can hell so abide within? How can there be a hell where heaven so resides," queried the bishop as his brow furrowed in complexity.

"As you will see..." he replied, watching as the dark portal opened of its own volition to admit the two.

"Heaven does not exist apart from itself. Know that what you are about to witness is a condition of purification. It is provided in the fullness of our Father's love for all – even the unrepentant souls. Yet, their journey lies more in a shadow than in the light."

The vision that confronted the bishop as they passed through the doorway was a scene to be forever etched to his soul. He felt the air escape from his chest like a torrent and he had to hold fast to Elijah's arm lest he fall to swoon.

The incredible power of the numerous vortices before him seemed to draw with great force the screaming souls stuck within. Each vortex seemed to bear malignancy. He could see decrepit and despairing souls trying to escape the power from which they were entrapped. Screams of misery filled the air from those clasped by the power of the vortex to which they were captured.

"In the name of God, to what do I bear witness?" he asked in despair of Elijah. "Why does God permit such torment of his children?"

"All men are brought face-to-face with a full account of that which stands within the consequence of their deeds," he replied.

"And who are those souls here," said the bishop pointing to the angelic-like beings standing in multicoloured robes in great numbers beside each of the vortices.

"Those are the angels-in-waiting. They are here to assist at the very moment a tormented soul can draw itself from its captivity within the vortex."

"And what, in the name of God, comprises these vortices of pain and suffering? Why can they not escape of their own volition?"

"These vortices you see are the design of the power of errant passion. Those souls, captured by the power of lust, envy, greed, wrath and gluttony, capture the unrepentant soul within its grasp. Even as some try to escape from its clutches, they are yet drawn back into its mire by clasping hands."

"Then, is this not God's judgement and wrath that so captures these poor souls?"

"No! Nothing could be further from the truth. God's wrath is but a figment of misguided stories and wayward religious doctrine. These souls are captured by their own choice. Greed, lust, malice and revenge are indelible snares that capture a soul within and hold it fast. That is until repentance unshackles the soul and embraces it with grace. Then, and only then, can the angels that you see in attendance come to aid the soul and remove it to restoration and healing."

The bishop could barely take his eyes from the suffering with which he was confronted, to take in the wisdom of law that Elijah had just described.

"But how long must a soul remain trapped by the power of such immense suffering?"

"At the first sign of contrition, the angelic souls to which you bear witness will remove the soul from the vortex to then minister their charge with the healing elixirs of God's grace."

"Does this mean that their sins are forgiven and are absolved from their transgressions?"

"No! Each soul must face the consequences of its actions. This is a divine law of heaven, as you now well know."

"Do you mean to say that this, to what I now bear witness, is merely a precursor to forthcoming atonement?"

"Can you think of anything else that would better describe the torment of hell?" replied Elijah.

Before the bishop could fain response, Elijah motioned that it was time to depart. "Come," he said firmly. "It is time to leave."

The bishop stood fixed to his spot and could barely exert enough strength to move a muscle.

"But why are you showing me these things?" he enquired. But he had turned only to see Elijah heading towards the open portal by which they had entered. He hastened to catch up, again.

The passage of time did not seem to matter. It felt to me as if time was no longer a construct of my eternal 'nowness'. I didn't need to be anywhere. It was as if perfection lay resident in each moment. I was not late for anything. *I mean*, I mused, *one could not be late for anything where time does not exist.* The thought brought a quaint smile to my face. Yet, I could not shake the feeling that there was more. More of what I could not yet determine. The thought lay just beyond the limits of my grasp.

Drifting, my thoughts returned to my recent past, as I sat in recline in the comfort of my house, where the pain of my life's experiences held me in thrall to suffering. Yet, now, the memories seemed to be liberated from the extent of my attachment. Yes, they were real, or at least they had been. But now they appeared as mere spectacle – without the claws. I could observe without remaining captive to their power and pain. These thoughts, once again, found a grin. "But, what now?" I asked aloud to the no one that was there.

As if in response to the immediacy of my thoughts, a voice echoed, in resonance, through my being.

"No person can ever cause you to regret your existence, or hate, or deny your Creator that I Am. Only you can allow those things to happen."

A spasm or jolt passed through me like a bolt of electricity. At once my surroundings seemed to fill with light. A light so bright that it was almost too much to bear, or bear witness to. I fell to my knees in supplication.

"But it is only me," I managed to mumble. "I am as nothing. Others are more deserving…"

I wasn't sure if it were a rumble or a residue of mirth, but the light seemed to grow brighter and the very essence I breathed seemed to fill with more divinity or love.

"To know that you are sacred is not to see new things in you, but to see yourself as you truly are," intoned the majestic voice. "If you could see yourself as I see you, you would smile, a lot."

"But why am I here? What was I sent to accomplish?" I asked, rising from my knees and staring out upon the extent of the ornate garden that was my own. Suddenly my outward vista began to change. What had been before seemed to transform before my eyes. My beautiful garden, the house, all was in transformation. But I could not yet determine to what.

"Come, let me show you," commanded the beautiful voice.

It wasn't until reaching a small pool served by a gentle stream that Elijah stopped and turned to speak to his charge. The bishop noted his new surroundings in a glance. He stood panting and relieved to be anywhere but where he had recently been. Even this small dot of pleasure in heaven's wide expanses proved abject relief from the pain and suffering he had just witnessed.

"Come," said Elijah as he motioned to sit under the shade of an overhanging branch beside the grassy bank of the gently flowing stream. "We should repose a while. After such as you have witnessed, your spirit requires revival."

Both sighed in unison as they sat and inhaled the sweet air of elixir and watched the fish swim effortlessly with the currents in the stream, unperturbed by any sense of predator or peril, merely in league with the flow that gave them direction.

The bishop could hardly hold himself upright, such was his sense of exhaustion. Yet, the questions were causing a logjam in the back of his head and, despite his fatigue, he could not resist but to give them a voice, turning to look at his friend and mentor. "Why? Why do those souls undergo such torment?" he voiced, still captive to the dolorous images of the vortices.

"That healing is found in the middle of suffering is an inviolable law of heaven and earth," intoned Elijah.

"What?" replied the bishop with more ire and angst than he meant to portray. "Do you mean to tell me that a soul's suffering is the pathway to the gates of heaven?"

"Suffering, no!" replied Elijah as he errantly drew geometric circles with a stick in the sand between where they sat. "Suffering is a construct of the mind that creates it. But surrender, my friend, is another matter. Surrender is the ending of the two and the opening of the one."

Aghast and unwilling to concede his incredulity, the bishop continued to argue.

"Do you mean to tell me that we have to give up? That we need forestall attainment, to concede our desire for enlightenment, our pursuit to realise the divine? Surely it cannot be so?"

"Not at all. The quest for enlightenment is the crucible's mixture to the alchemist. Yet, surrendering to the hand of God as

He transmutes the base metal into gold is the key to realisation. God is the doer, my friend. Allow Him to be so."

The bishop sighed in deference to his friend's wisdom as Elijah continued to scratch his stick deep into the sand. "Ah, there you are!" he exclaimed with glee as he removed a rather long worm from beneath the sand at his feet. "Eat, my friends," he said with a smile as he tossed the long morsel into the stream and watched the many fish enjoy a very savoury repast.

Chapter Five

The Beginning

Have mine eyes ever beheld such wonder?
Wisdom of ages, knowledge unbound, truth revealed.
Seek and ye shall find,
Ask and it shall be received.

He that believeth in me, and abides my words,
Shall it be done unto he.
Our Father's kingdom so vast, His love boundless,
But rid your encumbrances afore ye can see.

Seek thee thy divine purpose?
Or, rest, repose in comfort shall it be?
Cast aside thy burdens of earthly bear,
Your divine unfolding awaits.

What you have sown lies at heaven's door,
Yet, by the power vested in He,
Open the door.
Enter unto thine glory – so be it.

With great care, Atticus took me gently around the waist, and with a flash we were both standing on a hilltop surrounded by lush flora and hues of colour that defied any earthly comparison. We both stood bearing witness to a great city. To me, as a young initiate to heaven's graces, I was so astounded by what had just happened I could barely mumble my amazement.

"How did you do that? I mean, we were just standing on the balcony of my home, and now, and now we are here." The last word was exclaimed in such a manner that Atticus could hardly restrain his mirth.

"My dear Athar," he said, "soon you too will understand our ways in heaven."

In reply, I could only manage to close my mouth that hung open by itself.

"In heaven, all things are created by thought. All form is the instrument and vehicle of consciousness. Thought is the creative force of the universe. It is no different on earth," he continued. "Everything on earth is a creation of thought. Only here, in heaven, it is instantaneous – as you think is as you create. If we choose to be somewhere, or with someone, it is by the power of loving-thought that it is so. What you see before you is the creation of great minds in cohort with the divine."

"But how?"

"Soon, my friend, you too will learn how," he affirmed as we started to walk towards the city.

"I will?"

"But of course! Think about it like this. When on earth you walked somewhere, did you have to tell your leg muscles to move in a certain manner? Did you have to remind your arms to swing in cadence with your stride?"

"No, of course not. They moved of their own accord."

"Indeed, and so it is with us here in heaven. With practice, you know what to do, automatically. You just need to harness the power. This power becomes exponential when worked in cooperation with other like-minded spirits for the benefit of others."

"Can you show me, please? I mean now. I am eager to learn."

"Yes, I know, my good Athar, for that is why we are here."

We both looked again in awe at the magnificence of the city, which we were now striding towards. Not to make light of the radiance of the city streets, byways and gardens, for it was a symmetry that bespoke of a grand design of great minds. To compare the greatest of earthly cities to this point of comparison would be like comparing the seed to the rainforest. Yet, standing central to this majesty was a structure so amazing to my sight, I could barely describe its splendour.

The colonnades standing as sentinels to support the building seemed not so much to be overly tall. Rather, they were stately, and they shimmered with an inner glow that resonated with a divinity of their own. It was as if they knew their living purpose and were happy to reveal such for all eternity. The colour of alabaster and the strength of marble would go some way to present a comparison. Even the overarching roof and eaves seemed to both draw forth the energy from the majestic surroundings, as much as they provided shelter for that which lay within.

"Come," said Atticus with a prompt, "there is much more for you to see."

As we both moved up the steps and into the wide vestibule, it was all I could do but fall to my knees. Not so much in amazement, but most certainly in awe. Statues of the many great Masters of learning over the millennia stood proud and regaled as greeters to all who entered.

Entering through the ornate vestibule was an experience of itself, yet when I entered the grand hall, it was as if the whole of my world coalesced into the moment. Grand books, great tomes lined each wall. No space rested without a covering manuscript. Many desks, too many to count, were filled with students of all manner of shape and size in course of study. The numerous masters and teachers in attendance were at the call for those students deep in the throes of learning.

To break open my stupor, Atticus proffered his hand to guide me forward.

"Here, in the great hall of learning, resides all of the great wisdom found within the universe," he explained. "All resides as knowledge for those willing to open their heart and mind to the wisdom of the ages." Glancing at my eagerness he added,

"Go, we have but time. Explore to your heart's content. I will leave you in the capable hands of the master librarian."

Having spoken such, with a flash, too quick to perceive, Atticus was no longer by my side, only to be replaced by one who only can be described as a grand scholar. His long beard reaching down did little to hide the brightness of his enfolding robe. Yet, it gave resonance to his eyes with a light that seemed to reach into the depths of great wisdom.

"Here in the great hall resides wisdom and love expressed to word. For the sum of these elementals produce divine reason," said he in a voice that resonated like a drumbeat to my soul. "I am known by many names. Some you have heard across the many years of earth history. But you can just call me, Master Librarian," he said with a hint of a smile disguised under his flowing beard of white.

Given the state of my awe, I could barely summon words of gratitude for my presence in the great hall. I knew my mouth was working, but I could not summon the proper words. It mattered not, however, for it seemed he could read the heart of my thoughts without the verbal necessities.

"I understand that your heart is full of the desire to learn the ancient arts of healing, is that not so?"

Wrenching my attention from the many tomes, I could but stare at his insight to my heart of hearts.

"I, ah, well, yes, yes, it was, I mean, it is. But my life... I was, ah, held back, by my, by my..."

"It requires no explanation, my child. All has been revealed to me by Atticus, and it is the love of the Father that has brought you here. Your story sits well within the cauldron of our Father's love, I but his servant. And, I would add, you are most welcome any time to the grand hall, as your journey progresses." He just smiled as he spoke with a light that seemed to cast his eyes in some inner glow of knowing that I could not comprehend.

"Come," he said, as he led me along a passageway replete

with pictures of the great minds of the ages. As we entered the room devoted to the science of healing, he pointed toward a particular tome. "I recommend you begin with that book over there."

Almost without conscious thought, I was beside the bookcase and rifling through the many pages of great healing practices and learning. Then, without consciousness of passing events, I looked up to the Master Librarian with a look of both astonishment and incredulity.

"But within this tome is both knowledge of the past… and the future. Not currently known on earth. How is this so?"

Taking a few steps forward and placing a solemn hand to my shoulder, he explained, "We here are the custodians of truth. Truth does not care what we choose to believe – it remains unchanging. It stretches both before the now and into the now."

"But that is amazing! Should but a minuscule of this knowledge be fulfilled on earth, it would change the lives of many for the better."

"A wise utterance, my young learner. And what would you do with such knowledge should you be presented with such opportunity?"

"Why, I would help many who were beset with illness and malady. Those many who suffer under the yoke of pain and malaise from abuse, maltreatment and shattered innocence."

"This is a grand purpose you have bespoken, young soul. Do you wish it to be so? Would you so enlighten the many with such a divine purpose?"

Despite my naivety of how the many things worked here in heaven, I took little time to respond.

"Yes," was all I could muster with an earnest heart.

The Master Librarian thus smiled and turned as Atticus entered the room just at that same moment.

"I think our young Athar is ready for the beginning of his divine purpose."

To such a revelation, Atticus' smile was as deep as his knowing.

"Elijah," implored the bishop, "you have shown me many things, and I am much in your debt…"

"Hold, hold it right there," replied Elijah butting in. "Here, in heaven, there is no system of debit or credit. Nothing is ever measured via zero-sum in the house of the Father. Here we only 'serve'. Service to others is our reason for being. It is via this pathway to divinity that we evolve to the higher echelons of our Father's kingdom."

The bishop's confusion was plain to see, and it took a few moments to process the depth of meaning of the words.

"Is there more? More than what I have already seen?"

"Much more, my dear Bishop. Even more than I am yet to fully embrace… But this is for another time," he said, looking into the far distance with a heart open to the graces yet to be revealed. "Come, I will show you as much as I can. It is time for you to relieve some of those burdens that still cling to you from your life on earth."

At this, Elijah marched at a quick pace towards a series of rolling hills. For his part, the bishop could only hasten behind to catch up, again.

"Ah, there she is," indicated Elijah with a pointed finger. "That is her house, there."

The bishop looked down the dale at a small church, not much dissimilar to ones he had seen within his own See. It was small, but it was sturdy. Its walls of wood and whitewashing bespoke of tender hands to its creation, with the cross upon its entrance steepling and speaking much about what lay within.

As they stepped upon the small vestibule leading to the open front door, the bishop could hardly repress his astonishment.

"I know this woman," he exclaimed as he tugged on the sleeve of Elijah's robe to halt his progress.

"Yes," exclaimed Elijah, "she has recently arrived. Her life on earth has completed and she is here now, as you see."

"Sophia, it is I, your Bishop," he said taking a large stride toward the woman who was kneeling before the large cross positioned on the wall at the end of the hall. But, despite the bishop's effusive greeting, the woman did not seem to hear. This time it was Elijah who restrained the bishop's enthusiasm with a warning hand to his sleeve.

"She cannot hear you," he explained.

"But why? I do not understand. She was a devout parishioner. She attended church every Sunday. She was always the first in line to receive the sacrament."

"Indeed, she was. Yet, now, here, she is held fast by fear. Her fear holds her in binds yet to be broken."

"Fear, how? Of what? Our Father's kingdom is vast. His love boundless."

"My dear Bishop, what you see is a soul bound to the thralls of Judgement Day. Since crossing over, she remains steadfast in her fear of being judged by our heavenly Father. It is what she has learned. What she was told from the pulpit." He paused to gaze with loving compassion upon the still kneeling woman. "She fears greatly that her 'sins' on earth offer her no chance of redemption other than hell's eternal fire. She is closed to all the love and compassion awaiting her opened eyes. Her mind is fixed upon what she was told as truth. It is the lodestone she has brought with her across the veil. Yet, as you have seen, this is not the heaven that is real."

Looking still aghast, the bishop could only mumble, "But surely there is some way to help her? To break the yoke of her servitude to falsehood."

Elijah did not speak further words, but the look he gave the bishop bespoke a thousand of the same. Hesitantly, then, it must be said, did the bishop walk slowly forward. He too remained tacit as he knelt beside the still kneeling woman who hadn't raised her eyes from the cupped hands of her prayers.

"Father," he said as he too held his hands to prayer. "Please it be to shine your love upon this your child. Through my ignorance, I cannot help her. Through that which she was wrongly taught on earth, has her life now in heaven become a prison to her spirit. Help her. Please let it be so."

Not noticing it before, but now, upon these words, did the bishop feel the soft caress of a gentle breeze move as a mystery through the apertures of the small abode. Then, with the soft flow of her hair as if taken by a subtle breath, Sophia raised her head from her hands ever so slightly. From his prone position, the bishop could just see the hint, or was it a flash of light behind her eyes. Perhaps it was the reflection from the cross upon the wall. Whatever it was, it was enough, because that was when Elijah came silently behind the bishop and gently clasped his shoulder. He too did not say anything, just motioned with his eyes toward the two divine beings now stationed inside the door. One of the divine beings stepped forward and intoned, "Thank you, Bishop. We will take it from here."

As they moved outside, both Elijah and the bishop stood in awe of the glow of light that emanated from inside the church. It was then that the bishop happened to look down at his robes. He noticed with a quaint smile that much of the greyness had since been replaced. In its stead was a burgeoning, vibrant colour of blue. Not all, mind you, but certainly in alteration for the better.

In his usual staccato way, Elijah just said, "Come, it is time for us to go. She is now well served by our Father's hands."

Turning one last time to glance toward the young soul, the bishop could hear the words spoken in choral by the two attending angels,

"Benedicat te omnipotens Deus."

He smiled well, for he knew these words to be etched for eternity on his own heart.

Chapter Six

The Great Divide

Stand upon the precipice – afore thy gates of pearl,
Fear greatly – will thee fall to death?
Return ye cannot, forward succours thee not,
What shall it be?

Listen, whispers the ethers,
I am here with thee.
Trust, follow the music in thy heart,
Let you fall, I will not – open thine arms to Me.

Cleansed am I by repentance?
Absolved of sins, am I?
Nay, I say, yet, the door has opened,
The way is clear.

Be not deceived,
God is not mocked.
Abide to the words ever whispered to your ears,
Open your heart – I am as close to you as to Me.

We strolled, did Atticus and I, only breaking the serenity of the moment with words we thought the most important. Despite the lushness of the vista through which we traversed it was still hard for me to reconcile my soul's bearing within the context of my previous experience. Finally, though, did I manage to break open the confines within my tumbled thoughts to voice that which was most pressing.

"Atticus, how is it that I have been thus blessed?"

On pause, Atticus did smile gently at whom he had so

attended with love yet knew there was much more for me to discover.

"I mean, I was so lost before the bishop came to my succour. I was at once bound by my anger and guilt that I could not see. But now, I look to behold the majesty of God's graces." The wave of my arm did much to anoint the vast display of colours and varied hues within the splendour of the vista. It was as if each tree and blade of swaying grass was alive to the prospect of the moment. *Ah, behold! Two divine souls do approach*, they seemed to chant in chorus. It is time for us to spread our love.

Whilst acknowledged with a half-smile that creased the corner of his eyes, Atticus could only remain cryptic as his stride took a pace towards a destination unknown to my naivety.

"Love is a strong elixir, Athar. Anyway, who is the more deserving among us? Those who profess to know the mind of God, and sow seeds of self-righteousness. Or those who bear the weight of false doctrine making life, and life eternal, more difficult by such misplaced virtue."

My look of confusion did much to demonstrate my conundrum. So much so, that Atticus had to explain that his laugh was not meant as derision, rather in ease to the burden upon my soul – for he knew the answer would be presently revealed.

As if then by some unknown hand, Atticus stopped abruptly, only to stand in attention to something unseen.

"Listen," he said. "Can you hear it?"

The shake of my head was my only precursor to a higher calling of attention.

"Yes, yes, I think so. It is soft, like a lullaby. Only, only of more comfort."

Again, Atticus could but barely restrain his smile when I strode towards the crest of the hill to hear more clearly.

"Yes, yes, I hear it now. The music, it is so, so... beautiful," I exclaimed in awe as my visage reflected the grace that fell upon my ears. I turned then away from the music to ask further of what I beheld, but Atticus was no more. He had gone.

The rise of fear that found course to my heart was only momentary, for the words of my guide spoke clearly through the ethers.

"Go forward, my friend. Follow the music. It will lead you to where you are meant to be. Fear not, you are never without the love of our Father."

My deep inhale of the surrounding precious elixir made fast the tremor of my heart, and I took a forward step to follow that which I could not resist. The music became louder, more luxurious the closer I got to the apex of the hill that I scaled. Then I came to an abrupt halt... right on the very edge of the precipice.

All at once, it felt as if all the demon terrors of heaven and earth had been unleashed to my torment. The swirling mist that had suddenly descended from the unknown did not help, either. It seemed to hold fast to conceal all that lay before and beyond my proper senses. I could neither see my way forward nor my path of retreat.

"Atticus, where are you? Why have you led me to this place?"

This entreat only echoed through the mists to rebound in profound silence. But, girding my loins and summoning crumbs of courage, I inched forward, not knowing what lay before me.

"God, help me," I cried. "I don't know what to do."

Then, as if it were no more than a whisper, a soft breeze caressed my cheeks and the swirling mist cleared, at least enough to reveal what lay before me. It was enough to make me startle in absolute terror. I felt my heart bound swiftly into my mouth when I viewed the grand chasm before me.

The depth of the cavern could be by no means ascertained, even when my foot inadvertently crumbled the edge for the rocks to tumble down without a sound. One more false step would see me catapult down to depths unfathomable. Even my faint sense of bravado did nothing to ease my burdens of fear.

"It's not the fall that hurts you," I said out loud in hope that someone would hear my pretence at mirth. But my reasoning told me that the harsh bottom of the cavern would have a great deal to say about the outcome if I tumbled forward.

Just as I resolved to turn about to retrace my steps to safer ground, the mist seemed to separate of its own volition. I could but watch in awe and expectation of what was being revealed. I could see it on the other side of the wide expanse. It shimmered with an ethereal glow that could only be the magnificence of the God whose hand created it. The pillars of the gates shimmered like pearls upon the sea, and the radiance of the white columns could do nothing else but inspire admiration. I had been told something about these gates when I was in seminary, but rarely did I pay it much heed at that time. It seemed like wild fantasy and told from the lips by those who only professed to know by rote of learning, not by depth of experience. Yet here they were. Standing open before me. But I could not cross. The chasm was too wide, the cavern too deep to traverse.

Yet despite my augmenting fear mixing with not a small amount of frustration, I could not resist the feeling that I HAD to cross. Even from this distance, I could see that the shimmering gates were ajar. There was no lock, nothing barring my entrance, apart from the chasm before me. Beyond the open portal, I could even discern the construction of a large mansion set amidst an acreage of the lush flora, in colours too vivid for my mind to grasp without desire. It was even grander than the home to which I had recently become accustomed. Maybe this was my home? My real home? I turned to look back from where I had come, and it was as if my whole life flashed before me in review. It felt like the inside of a kaleidoscope passing in an instant. I couldn't help it! I didn't intend the profane, but the words just came out.

"Holy shit! That sure was one tough road," I exhaled deeply

into the ethers.

But it was right about then I knew what I had to do. Or, at least, what I wasn't going to do. I knew I wasn't going back. I couldn't go back.

A deep inhale gave me enough strength to at least turn back to face the chasm and the dilemma that confronted me. Staring ahead in complexity, I felt another soft touch of breeze caress my rendered spirit. It somehow gave me strength. Then, as if from everywhere and nowhere at the same time, the music again resounded like a beating cadence in my heart.

"Trust. Let go. You are worthy," the music seemed to say with a resonance that tickled my innermost sanctum.

Maybe this was what all that struggle was about, I reasoned. It seemed to be the final stanza. I was leaving behind the residue of my endless torment and pain for this, the beginning of a new life of eternal – well – bliss. At least that is what the Good Book had said. I remembered reading that part and it had stayed with me across the veil.

Lost love, betrayal, grief, and endless pain! No one could have scripted how my life had turned for this small, insignificant human droplet in the ocean of other sentient beings. *Hey, it's just little ol' me,* I thought with servitude to my past, standing on the edge staring at the gates on the other side. *Do I deserve this? Am I worthy?* The questions seemed innocuous enough – but no answer seemed forthcoming as I stood looking across at my eternal endpoint.

Again, the same music played loud to my ears as I stood not knowing how to go forward, but unable to turn to reverse.

"I guess I've got no other choice. I must trust. I have to 'let go'," I said into the still swirling mists.

My full attention turned forward with a resolution, but even then, I had to squeeze my eyes firmly shut. Of their own volition, my arms opened wide as I took a step forward. The eternity of the second it took for my foot to move was enough to expect my toppling over and descent into the abyss.

Thud! I heard the sound echo as I felt the reassurance of the solid foundation beneath me. I opened my eyes as my hands felt the surety of stone. "It was there all the time. Why is it that I did not see?" I gasped as I looked across the bridge that spanned the divide and prevented my fall. I couldn't help it. I started to laugh. A laugh that started in my mind but finished in my belly.

"I did it! I trusted! I let go!" I yelled. "And I'm still alive... well, here anyway."

I looked across the span towards the entrance portals as I strode forward with purpose. Even from a distance, I could see the resonance of his shimmering cloak. It seemed to possess more colours of the rainbow than I could begin to describe or remember from so recent a viewing.

"Welcome," Atticus said, as he opened his arms in joyous greeting. "I've been waiting for you."

This time I didn't hesitate. I hastened forward and could feel the waves of love from his heart the nearer I approached.

"Why did I take so long?" I asked when swept into the overwhelming grace of Atticus' angelic embrace.

"It matters not," was his reply with a smile. "You are home now. Your Father awaits."

The bishop felt still a little dumbfounded by his reacquaintance with Sophia. So much so that he could only watch absently, when distracted by a small bird as it flitted amongst the flowers, so nearby the large tree against which both he and Elijah reclined. It must also be said that the many varieties and hues of radiant flowers and evergreens were doing their best to exude all the most beautiful of essences and vitality. They even hummed a soft tune in a joyous union that Elijah most enjoyed, yet it made little impact upon the bishop's downcast demeanour. Finally, to relieve his friend of his stupor, it was Elijah who turned to his companion.

"Why do you lament so? God's hand dances well upon your soul. Your journey is enlivened by His grace."

"Elijah, I muse upon the many heinous mistakes I made in life. The more I learn of heaven and its works, the more it seems by my ignorance have many in life been misguided by my words and hubris."

"Much that you have seen thus far is to refute much that you taught and upheld during your priestly life, that is certain. Is this why you lament so?" he replied.

Saying this, almost absentmindedly, Elijah turned to watch a little bird in its play amongst the branches, and then calmly held out his hand. Taking one look, the little creature seemed to know his intention, to speed straight toward the outstretched welcome. Its tweet of contentment and curiosity was enough for them both to titter in surprise.

"You try," said Elijah.

"Me?" replied the bishop, as if it were a request of the impossible.

"Sure! How do you know you cannot if you do not try?"

With some sense of hesitation, the bishop held his hand forward as an invitation. The little bird's tweet explained that he knew more than was given credit. So he duly hopped from Elijah's hand across to that newly proffered, with his tweet explaining his satisfaction.

"You see," said Elijah, "the bird understands."

"It does?"

"Yes, of course!"

Suddenly, the bird flew to land gently upon the bishop's shoulder. Where he continued to tweet his song into his ear.

"But what does that have to do with my life as Bishop, and how the limitations of my knowledge of the laws of heaven have impeded many of those I sought to relieve?"

"God would have all men be saved, my dear Bishop. None shall be left behind. Yet, it is so that as a soul is before its moment of passing, is exactly as it is upon arrival here in heaven. True repentance at the time of death leads only to open the door to our Father's love. It does not absolve wrongdoings. The law of 'what you have sown, so shall you reap' is inviolate – even in the face of the fear of death. Fervent adherence to erroneous doctrines has caused many to remain unaware of God's true laws of love."

At once, and most suddenly, did the tiny bird fly from the bishop's shoulder. Yet he did not fly away. Rather, he fluttered in front of his face and made effort to extort him to follow.

"I think the little one means us to follow," intoned Elijah with a knowing smile.

Following down dale and across a gentle stream, they followed the bird and, even when lost to sight, they could follow its call through an ever-deepening forest. At once, the thickness and tangle of the flora became so dense that they had to manoeuvre the leaves and branches aside to make their way. There was no discernible path to follow, yet the bird's song remained clear to their passage. With such rough trail, it even seemed they traversed for many miles. Then, suddenly, as if by sleight of hand or force of will, they entered upon a clearing. In amidst of this clearing stood another church, but this one was much larger than that before encountered.

Despite its magnitude, its whitewashed walls of wood stood like a beacon amongst the dense greenery of its surroundings. From inside could be heard the soft murmur of ardent prayer mixed with the stringent essence of strong incense. It did, to the bishop, remind him much of his former life. Turning back toward Elijah, he opened his mouth to voice such surprise, but before he could bring thoughts to words, the little bird flew towards the closed door of the church, to flitter and chirp his intention. He wanted them to enter. The door even opened ajar of its own accord to admit the two and, as soon as they stepped across the threshold, the little bird flew to attend in the waiting trees. Swinging open with a creak, the portal opened upon the expanse of the nave to reveal that which lay within. The bishop could hardly contain his astonishment.

Many souls with heads bowed in prayer sat in the rows of pews aligned before the giant cross fixed upon the end of the hall and behind the marble altar. It felt as if the bishop had returned home. Without any hesitation, head held high, and hands placed in benediction, he strode with purpose down the aisle. When reaching the altar, he turned to gaze with pleasure at the many bowed heads of the congregation.

"Raise your heads, my brethren. It is I, your Bishop, who has returned to your side."

Yet, even upon these words, not one head did raise from its prostration. The bishop was crestfallen. Neither through raised voice nor exhortation could he make his presence known to those in need of his words. Eventually, depleted and dejected, he gave up. He could expend no further effort.

Still standing stoically, Elijah watched all as the scene unfolded.

"Why do they not abide me?" extorted the bishop. "I am their Bishop, am I not?"

Without a word, Elijah walked the aisle to aid the bishop from his dilemma. Taking his hand gently, he led his glum friend back to the entranceway, whereby they positioned to sit upon the stairs of the vestibule of entry.

"This is a harsh lesson for you, Bishop. What you now witness is a great divide between what you before believed and now what you know."

"But why? Why have I been so chastened? My intent was always to bring seekers to the Lord. It was as proclaimed in the Bible. I, merely its chosen messenger. What is wrong with these people?"

"A soul's fervent adherence to a particular religious practice will continue to weigh upon them until they become enlightened with the spirit of love. Oft-times, it is easier to be a religious follower than a spiritual voyager."

The bishop squirmed somewhat uncomfortably on his seat as if dawning knowledge made him further ill at ease. "Now I know the result of my lack of understanding and self-righteousness. But how are such bigotry and misguided prejudice to be undone?"

Elijah looked upon his friend with great compassion before he spoke. "When you were before in earnest trying to make the people listen to you, what did you hear?"

"Nothing! I heard nothing. Except for the sound of my lament," he added.

"Exactly?"

"But I do not understand."

"Come, let us try again. Go again to the altar... but this time, listen. Listen for the words that ring plainly from your heart to your ear."

The bishop followed the instructions and traversed the aisle to the altar, but this time he stood and listened. At the very same instant, the little bird flew directly through the open door to perch itself, once again, on the bishop's shoulder.

"Tweet, tweet," was the bird's discourse into the bishop's attending ear. Then, as if a light illumed behind his eyes, the bishop stood enraptured.

"God, save us from hell's fire! Forgive us our sins!" was the chant that the bishop could now plainly hear with open ears.

Then as if through a wave of insight, his face expressed that which to his mind was now clear.

"They think that their heavenly reward is deliverable by their earthly adherence to worship every Sunday."

Elijah's nod was enough to offer as confirmation.

"Importantly, they do no harm, either to themselves or their neighbour, for they remain a community unto themselves. Yet, no pressure is ever brought upon these souls. Their resurrection must come from within. They must see beyond the confines of the dogma that has ensnared them in blindness."

"But how? When?"

Then, in answer, the little bird reappeared, but this time with many of his friends. So many, that the very air much tremored with the flap of their wings. Being most favoured, the little fellow once again alighted on the bishop's shoulder. Only this time the tweeting was understood by the listener.

"We attend for but a spark, even a flicker. God would have it that all men be saved. Your presence here, dear Bishop, may just be that spark. No love ever goes to waste."

At this, the little bird flew into the surrounding trees with all his friends. Neither Elijah, nor the bishop, had to listen hard to hear the cadence of tweeting-in-wait for the spark of divinity that love had created.

Chapter Seven

The Great Gardens

All men are to be saved,
Exceptions there are none.
Thy will be done, but how?
If I know not my purpose.

Asleep, are they? If I may inquire,
Burdened and afeared, maybe.
Awaken the sleeper to thy new abode,
To rest secure in His hands.

Your soul's journey begins anew,
Feast upon abounding love.
Know deprivation not,
Spirit guides, never misguide.

Grieve not for those who remain,
Seek first to know.
Know who guides your hand,
Know who lights your way.

Standing upon the balcony of the new abode I now call home, I could but marvel upon that which I observed. Much stood to my amazement, none more so than the robe in which I was now attired. It had transformed to luminance. It seemed to shimmer with light and lightness. Flashes of blue and yellow emanated from its folds as I moved limb or torso. Standing nearby, Atticus stood silent to allow the majesty of the present moment to bear witness to his friend's transformation.

"Atticus, how? Why?" I asked, not entirely knowing how to

complete my questions. But it mattered not, for my mind was known to his even before the questions were posed.

"To cross the bridge, my dear Athar, you must be cleansed. All errant traces of earthly life past must be washed clean from your spirit. As you have now been well acquainted, the colour of your attire is an indication of the condition of the wearer. No soul can enter the gates stained with the remnants of life's previous encumbrance. You have entered the next level of heaven's seven divinities. Even then, as you have seen, it takes great trust for each soul to complete such a leap of faith."

Standing as I did in awe of the beauty and grandeur before me, it felt to the newly arrived that I was ready to embark on a greater journey – yet knew not the vast expanse to be traversed.

"And am I free to come and go as I please? Is it possible to return across the bridge to those in need of love and guidance?"

"Of course it is, my dear friend. Come, let me show you."

With a gentle touch, Atticus guided me around the other side of the great house to a vantage point from which we could observe. Even from this distance, we could see many radiant souls making the traverse back to and from the other side.

"Where do they go?" I inquired.

"Each soul has a well-defined purpose and will minister love to those souls in need. Some will aid the sick and poorly of spirit. Others will attend those in greeting who have recently passed. Many are those who require succour from their attachments and addictions of life. Each soul passing over the bridge holds the light of our Father's love in their hands to fulfil His word – 'that ALL men are to be saved'."

"May I, I mean, can I begin such ministry?" I asked in earnest.

"Of course, there is much for you to do, my dear friend. Much that you will do to serve our Father. Indeed, there is ever much that needs be done for our Father's will to be done on earth as it is in heaven."

I could barely contain my enthusiasm for the task ahead, but

Atticus placed a restraining hand upon my shoulder to curb the eagerness of my intent.

"But first, let us walk through the majesty of the garden that now attends us. There is much that I would show you before you embark on your missions."

Elijah was greeted like a long-lost soul as they entered through the large gates bordering the estate. Many pleasant souls came to express their joy at his return and sought his attention and wise counsel. It was as if a stranger had returned from a long journey and whose presence was much missed by those who loved him dearly. Many hands guided him forward into the building's inner sanctum. He turned to look over his shoulder with an expression of resignation bordered by humility. *It said much to describe the innermost sympathies of his heart*, thought the bishop with a wry smile in return.

Greeted by such opportunity to wander and observe his current surroundings, the bishop strolled through the lush gardens of the manor they had entered. The gardens, well-manicured as they were, seemed to exude an essence that invigorated every moment. The numerous flowers and trees each seemed to sing a chorus of 'welcome' and 'be at peace'. The bishop, casting a glance at the gentle flower still resting in his lapel, could have sworn that the petals themselves had rejuvenated in the presence of its many kindred blooms. He even noted the tint of a blue haze that seemed to permeate the very air with a healing grace, the more one inhaled of its essence. He made mental note to ask of its composition to Elijah.

Out and spread amongst the gardens were an array of couches, much like those to which he had borne witness at the magnetic chorale. Each lounge contained a soul in repose. They were asleep. In attendance upon these sleeping forms were many beautiful souls, each walking by and in strict attention to the sleeper. They seemed each to be attired similarly in robes of the colouration of turquoise, or a shade of green that was well beyond what his eyes were attuned to on earth. Yet, others in attendance seemed to be dressed in all manner of shade and hue. Some were patiently reading, while others were engaged in animated conversations. For the bishop, not being able to hold his questions in, he approached with deference one of the attendants.

"Excuse the interruption," he asked, "but what is the matter with these souls? Why do they sleep? Are they okay?"

The attendant's smile was indeed broad in welcome. "You are not interrupting by any means, my friend. I am glad to answer your inquiry. These souls at rest are recent arrivals to heaven. Many of these cherished beings endured great maladies before their crossing over. Their illness before passing has had a debilitating effect on the soul. It needs rest to recover before assimilation into heaven's abode."

"And what, if I may inquire, is your role in such regard?"

"After their rejuvenation and upon awakening, many of these souls are in earnest, wishing to return to loved ones and kin still in the clutches of grief. Yet the cord is broken. There is nothing to be achieved by going back. They are attended assiduously by we who provide care and guidance."

"And who are these others who also wait patiently in attendance, yet seem to be not so occupied to such loving purpose?"

"Oh, but they will soon be called upon for a great service. For they are the known family of the recently departed. As soon as possible upon awakening, the newly arrived will be delivered to the hands of loving kin to forward their journey."

The attendant glanced to notice a faint murmur from one of the sleeping forms.

"Please, if you will excuse me, I must attend an awakening soul. He revives and will need guidance to assimilate to his currency and abode."

Moving calmly to stand beside the reviving form, the bishop asked, "May I stay? May I observe? I will not be in the way."

"Of course, you can," said he with a smile. "With the grace of our Father's love in your heart, it can but augment to his well-being."

The bishop could barely restrain his enthusiasm for the task of watching the unfolding events. Although it must be said, he did his best to stay unobtrusive and out of the way as many other attending souls came to offer support to the awakening soul.

From his position, the bishop could not discern each word of discourse, but it was plain to see the care and loving attention the soul received upon awakening. It seemed as if by thought, rather than word, that each attendant knew the exact requirements of the reposing soul's needs. To this awakening soul's initial surprise, upon opening his eyes, his demeanour changed suddenly to high agitation and unease. The best the bishop could discern was that the poor soul was not convinced that he had indeed passed and that there was no longer any means by which he could return to his grieving loved ones. After some moments, however, the attendants were able to satisfy him as to his safety and care. Then, upon espying his long-lost kin from amongst those standing in wait – seeing those he loved, changed his demeanour for the significantly better. Tears of joy and relief replaced a visage fixed previously in disquiet.

Watching in awe of the unfolding events with a tear close to his eye, the bishop neither noticed nor heard Elijah's quiet approach. So much so, that he startled at the familiar voice and gentle clasp to his shoulder.

"And so, this soul's journey begins anew. He is loved and in loving hands."

"But do you ever make mistakes? Can it be so that a misdiagnosis is made to a soul's detriment?" enquired the bishop in earnest.

"No, this is never possible. Although, it should be said that for some souls, the feelings of profound loss and grief by those who remain on earth are a force of attraction that is strong for some departed souls to resist."

"Do you mean to say that the grief of kindred on earth can be a hindrance to a departed soul?"

"As you have seen, dear Bishop, our Father's love and care for each of His children are without bounds. All souls are tended by His loving hands. If grieving kin knew the tender mercies of our Father, they would not need to lament their passing and parting to His care."

"But you never misguide, or act in error?"

"In heaven's hall, my dear friend, whatever is done for love's sake cannot be mistaken."

"Amen to that!" replied the bishop in confirmation and smile.

Chapter Eight

The Planning

Return must I,
Undo my wrongs, speak the truth.
Ears must hear that which is divinely true,
And that which is false.

All takes place within natural laws,
Seek first to understand.
Know the truth,
Else expand the lie.

No child left behind, shall they be,
All guided to their prime.
Our Father's gift bears the parents' responsibility,
His bond of love unbreakable.

Let thy tears flow, sweet child,
Your burdens are relieved.
Welcome to my hall, dear one,
As I AM, so shall you be.

It wasn't so much that he felt tired, it was more that he was overwhelmed. His energy had sunk as low as his spirits.

"Would that I could go back, to return to incarnate life and make right that which I had previously misdirected," said the bishop as they both reclined on the banks beside a gently flowing stream, the cool water into which they dangled their toes in delight. "I carry a heavy burden of trouble for that which I have done in ignorance to the truth."

Rummaging around, the small, flat pebble wasn't hard for

Elijah to find. He clasped it gently then tossed it into the pond to watch it skip many times across the expanse of water. So many times, in fact, it was impossible to count. The bishop could only look on in amazement. He remembered as a lad how he could only conjure at the most six bounces before his flat stones were lost to the depths.

"Those deeds committed in ignorance or without intention are not weighed to balance in heaven, dear Bishop. Only those who have erred with deliberate intent, or determined self-interest to another's detriment or negligence, are committed for their rightful consequences."

"Yet, it is so, by my teaching of false doctrine and insouciance to those under my care, I have left many in peril of their immortal soul. My glance in the mirror of reflection speaks to me with unease as to my forward progress in God's holy land. Is it possible to return to undo that which I have done?"

Elijah watched carefully the many and varied deep patterns of emotion that fell across the bishop's visage.

"To return is indeed possible, Bishop, but the circumstances upon which the journey is to be constructed require conditions and consultations from those higher above my station of evolvement."

"Yet it can be done?"

"Yes," replied Elijah with a hint of a smile hidden behind the frown of his brow. "But first, you must pass a great test. Then, and only then, can you take the next step toward such a contemplation."

The bishop's eagerness was akin to a small child about to visit a fairground. The very thought seemed to lift the weight of burden from his shoulders whereby his animation could barely be constrained. "What do I have to do. I will do anything. Anything you wish."

"So be it," said Elijah solemnly. "First, you must find a flat stone, much the same as the one I made dance to eternity across the waters."

Another flat stone wasn't hard to find, and the bishop proudly held it forth for examination. "Will this suffice to purpose?" he asked, holding it to the light and admiring its symmetry. To which he received a cursory nod.

"Now toss it into the water to see how many skips it will make."

The bishop felt the weight and flexed his arm in preparation. Recollections from his youth came flooding back to the art of the practice. He knew what to do. It was like riding a bike. He tossed the pebble into the water and stood in anticipation and expectation of the many skips of its journey. Alas, he fell most notably from his crest when the pebble could only manage five skips before descending into the depths.

Elijah's mirth at his friend's disappointment of the outcome was barely contained under his gruff exterior. Yet his eyes told an alternate story.

"Does this mean I have failed?" said the bishop in abject disappointment. "Does it mean that I cannot return to minister to those in need?"

"My friend, God shows us that all our errors and misdeeds can only delay, they cannot prevent, the ultimate realisation of the truth, our truth. Nothing ever takes place outside the natural laws. It is these laws you must seek to unravel before embarking on your expedition."

It was well known to the bishop that his friend was most eloquent both by word and deed, and he watched as Elijah bent down to pick up another flat pebble. He seemed to hold it in his hand for an extended time and even whispered words to the hard stone that the bishop was unable to interpret. Without so much as a practice swing, he tossed the pebble into the water and watched with a quaint smile its multitudinous skips across the water, well out of sight of eye's reach.

"But how? How did you do that?"

"Find another pebble, Bishop. But this time, speak to the pebble with love and devotion. Acknowledge its beauty. After all, it too is a reflection of God in heaven. Praise it as worthy and equal to the task of its journey."

The bishop, at first curiously, then with the dawning of wisdom, did so speak to the pebble held lovingly in his hand. Then, with a motion as fluid as the water into which it was cast, did he toss the pebble and watch with joy as it skipped upon the water to join its friends on the other side of eternity.

"Good," said Elijah as he clasped the bishop by the shoulder. "Now we can see to the next part of your journey. The return."

The two then cast a final glance across the expanse of water to where the pebbles were no more.

"Lead me on," said the bishop, with a mind still skipping across the water like a pebble.

"I have spent much time in the vaunted halls of the grand library," I said as I watched my guide and friend, Atticus, play joyfully with a bevy of small children around his knees. They sat around him in a half-circle and were happy to play and banter with the great man of wisdom.

"And what now do you feel, young Athar? What is your heart's desire?" he said, as a small child placed a beautiful flower in his lapel, for which she received a gentle smile and pat of thanks to her flowing locks.

"I am ready!" I exclaimed with only a small hint of pride. "My study has seen the growth of much wisdom. I am full to overflowing with the desire to share this knowledge on the earth with those in need."

Atticus rose from his seat and waved goodbye to his many young companions.

"Children, it is time to return to your instructions. I promise to join you presently for more of your games." The children, as one, seemed to understand. Then all, within but the blink of an eye, and each with a clasp of another's hand, just seemed to vanish.

My mouth had much trouble staying closed as I shook my head in bewilderment, but I still could not fathom a question that resembled common sense, about what I just witnessed.

"Let us depart, good Athar, I would show you another of our Father's havens replete with His glory."

With the gentle touch of his hand to my shoulder, we were immediately transported to the place of his desire. A place previously unknown to me, but awesome to my still-evolving understanding.

"You know, Atticus, I still cannot quite content myself with our mode of locomotion here in heaven. It seems so, so easy, yet it is so... unusual," I explained, seeking words to do my dilemma justice.

Smiling just as he does, Atticus replied, "It is much akin to riding a bike, is it not? Even the children can do it. But at first, it feels unusual, or uncommon, even. Yet, when accustomed, the spirit and mind know exactly what is required. Fear not, my friend, soon your thoughts will enable your motion with barely a thought. Now come, a new experience awaits your attention," he said, clasping me gently by the hand to lead me towards another magnificent edifice.

As we walked towards the luminous building, my astonishment almost overtook my etiquette, and I was not far removed from voicing an expletive in surprise.

"Atticus, there is my house, there over yonder, I can see it," I said, pointing. "It is just across the divide. I can see its vaunted windows and the grand garden. We are not far from the bridge of my crossing."

"Yes, that is so," he explained, as he continued toward the entranceway of the beautiful building to which he had directed us. I did most admire the joyous array of hues and shafts of rainbow colours that seemed to pervade the very atmosphere over and around the grand edifice. Even the air seemed to resonate with playfulness and delight that could but fill one's soul with elation to the spirit of God. As in many other places, the garden and many varieties of flowers played tickle with my senses, and it was easy to discern each item of flora singing in cadence with its colleagues. Every blade of grass and leaf of tree sang in joyous communion to those who attended their domain.

Inside, as we stepped through the vestibule, a vast array of rooms assailed our senses. Many containing enough space for a single dwelling for each resident. Each area was equipped with space enough for contemplation or study, and even repose. When entering further into the labyrinth, I heard the sound of many voices, children's voices. Not voices in overexcited eagerness, but rather in quiet enthusiasm for their tasks and actions. The sound was more akin to a quiet hum, rather than the boisterous cadence of a playground.

We passed a room, much like a library or classroom, where many students were under instruction from a master amidst a lesson of learning. Then, yet another large room containing many couches, similar to those previously described, held safe and secured many little souls in repose. It could be seen that many advanced beings were in close attendance to care for each sleeping form. I could barely contain my wonder as a myriad of questions tumbled to the fore and sought answers each before the other.

"Come," said Atticus, before I could find a proper voice. "There is someone I would like you to meet."

Moving further into the building's hallways, awaiting our attendance, was the most beautiful being I believe I had ever encountered.

"Atticus, it is good to see you, my old friend. I have heard much of the dominion of your love and good works." Her dulcet voice resonated in sweet cascade, then stopped as she cast her welcoming gaze upon me. It was as if I was showered in love by raindrops from the well of heaven. I did well to hold to my proper sensibilities but could find no words in proper greeting.

"I see that you have brought an eager student to our doors. Welcome..." she said as I clasped her outstretched hand in my own, feeling tingling through my being that I could not even now explain. "My name is Evangeline."

"Athar is an eager student of the divine, Evangeline, and has evoked a willingness to heal those in need and suffering. But first, I have brought him to your door to show the love and compassion that you minister to the children of heaven."

"I am most glad of your kindness, dear Atticus. And to you, Athar, I am at your service to explain how we minister to God's chosen innocents. Come, let us walk through the halls and I will speak with you of our Father's works."

At Evangeline's behest, we took a turn down a hallway, one of the many, and stopped at a large hall of study. It was a room filled with many tomes, not dissimilar to the great library of my previous visitations. The room was full of many eager young learners fixed in attention upon the master, amidst instruction at the front of the room.

"All children who have left the earth-plane in the early stages will continue their education and well-being. All shall receive proper instruction to the ways of heaven. No child shall be left behind in their education of the divine laws of heaven and earth. They are all, without exception, given the knowledge required to progress through the stages of the divine."

"But what of a parent's responsibility in such regard? Does not the bond between parent and child continue to blossom and hold fast to love and attachment?"

"Indeed, it does, Athar. The bond of love between a parent and child will extend across the eternal if only it is strong and true. No bond of love is ever broken. It is the cord that seeks to sustain one and the other across the vast expanse of our Father's heaven. Yet, if no such bond exists, if the strains of earthly relationships have soured such fulfilment, then, as you see, no child will suffer for its absence. Their well will be replenished by many loving hands so that the child knows not any privation."

I stood in awe perhaps a while longer than supposed – until Evangeline broke the spell of my fixation.

"Come," she said gently, "there is more for you to see."

We were led further along numerous hallways, each resplendent in fine décor and colourful design, until we arrived at another chamber that, even as we approached, seemed to resonate with a chorale of beautiful voices in quiet chant. The atmosphere held a faint tint of blue colouration which radiated through a window portal in the ceiling. It seemed to fill the very air with an elixir of life that held the potential for all love to flourish.

Inside the room, as we entered, I could not help but notice the glow of the number of souls in attendance to the many children. Each of their robes seemed to be alive with a radiance not before seen to my eyes, and their attention to the little babes under their care was evident to behold. Many young fledgelings lay in repose in the soft down of the vessel holding their comfort.

"Each child is a teardrop from the eyes of our Father, dear Athar. Each child is nurtured until they reach the fullness of their spirit. Their attainment of the prime of life is by no means hindered by their early passing to this heavenly realm. Our Father's love shines brightly upon each soul until it is of an evolvement to determine its future progress in the spirit of the divine."

As she spoke, without warning and of its own volition, my mind strayed to the many challenges and hurdles of my upbringing, and I could barely hold fast to my currency and to the love to which I now bore witness. Within but a beat, Evangeline seemed to know my thoughts in revelation.

"Your road has been difficult, dear Athar. This is known to us of the higher realms. Yet, know that the cross of your harsh learning is now akin to the alchemists' cauldron. What was before leaden, is now turning to the gold of joy and celebration to the task laying before you."

I couldn't help myself. I could no longer stand on any further ceremony. The joy in my heart was full to overflowing, and I reached out my hands to hers and fell to my knees as tears tumbled in heavy droplets upon my shimmering chemise.

"You are most welcome, my dearest Athar," she said helping me to rise. "But know that what I am – like these children – is what you too will become. And more so will it be."

Smiling upon these words, Evangeline took gracious leave and left me in awe, but with a heart replete. Alone in Atticus' company once more, as we made our way outside to the lush garden we stopped suddenly. I could not help but turn as we exited to see Evangeline standing by an open portal, to wave us good cheer in depart. My heart burst open again and I could not restrain another flood of tears that cascaded as before. It was as if a century of my harsh life had dissolved in a moment in the presence of such grace as I had just witnessed.

Atticus did not say anything. He did not have to.

Chapter Nine

The Naming

I come bearing a gift,
A gift of great import.
Acknowledge the beauty, say I,
What does't thou hear when thy name spoken be?

Surprise, I say? Nay.
One's name writs destiny's path.
Thy kingdom come, speaks to your name,
So let it be as anointed.

Behold, your key,
Sacred shall it be.
I give to you a name,
Be knighted to heaven, must you be.

Speak not thy name in vain,
But treasure the grace bestowed.
'Tis a gift a grace received,
This key to heaven's doors.

Sitting in repose and contemplation with his back placed firmly upon the trunk of a large tree of elm, the bishop was overlooking the vast beauty of the vista and expecting Elijah's soon return. He was startled to someone's presence by the soft clearing of a throat. But it was not Elijah.

"My apology to the interruption of your reverie," he said, "but I have come at the behest of our dear friend, Elijah. He has been called to another ministry and has asked for my attention to your assistance."

In the moments that abounded whilst he spoke, the bishop was able to take note of his description, although it should be said that nothing about his attire appeared diametric from the normal. His robe, although neatly flowing and radiant with a multitude of varying colours, seemed to contain subdued hues of a universal rainbow. No colour did dominate in deference to the other. Thus, the robe did not seem altogether different from the many he had seen in his travels in the land of spirit. Yet, there was something about his demeanour that made the tingles down his spine hard to explain.

"You do not interrupt at all, my friend. I was merely in contemplation of the beauty of the vista from across the dale. I still have difficulties in assimilating the vast magnitude and wonder of that which pervades," said the bishop, proffering his hand to gesture a seat beside him. "Please be at leisure and join me in such regard."

"I am most pleased to finally meet you, Bishop. I have been fortunate to have been made aware of your great progress, through the grace of Elijah."

Speaking thus, the bishop still could not place the distraction. It was as if he appeared more than he seemed.

"To what do I owe the courtesy of your visit, and by what name shall I address you?" asked the bishop.

"I am called Samuel, and I have come here not by chance, but rather bearing a special gift."

"A gift?" replied the bishop in surprise. "I confess to having received many surprise gifts since my arrival, although some more challenging and confronting than others, I have to say. But each a gift and surprise in their own right."

"Our land in heaven is ever a land of surprises. This is the majesty of our Father's kingdom. One knows where one has been yet knows not the vast expanse of the divinity that lays ahead. Such is, 'thy kingdom come'. If I but understand an inkling of our Father's grace, it is best to stay open to the magnitude of such surprises," Samuel replied, with a smile that spoke of a depth of knowledge and wisdom yet to be revealed.

"You speak truly, my friend," said the bishop as they lapsed into quietude in contemplation of all they beheld. Finally, Samuel broke open their reveries to speak more of the purpose of his visit.

"You have realised much since you transitioned to our realms, dear Bishop. But unknown to you as you traverse the various levels to heaven's higher divinities, you shed your earthly vestments of attachment and the sum of the consequences of your actions. It is important therefore that you are properly enabled."

The bishop's frown did much to explain his complexity. "Enabled? How? I thought, I mean, I have already been much blessed and can but thank our Father for His grace, given my lifelong ignorance and ignominy."

"Nonetheless, you are now in a state of consciousness in which you grow to realise your fullest potential. To continue thus you will need a key."

"A key?"

"Yes, dear friend, a key." At once Samuel stood erect, and with a helping hand, invited the bishop to do the same. In such an instant, his before nondescript robe seemed to morph into something altogether not before seen to the bishop's eyes. Samuel was radiant. What was before just an array of varied colours, now seemed to explode to a vast spectrum of blue, gold and white so that the bishop had to shield his eyes to pierce the divine aura. Taken aback as he was, he would have tripped upon a protruding rock, if not for the securing hand of Samuel's grasp.

"Behold, your key," he said, passing a roll of ancient parchment from his cloak into the bishop's outstretched hand. The old material made a crinkling sound as if unrolled from a time immemorial. What was written contained only one word scribed by a beautiful calligraphic hand:

Isaiah

The bishop could barely form a proper word and was only vaguely aware of the significance of the unfolding event. He felt transfixed as if hit by lightning, or a bolt from the divine. Try as he might in forming a point of reference from his previous life, he could not. The best he could assimilate was his time as a young boy when he first entered the grand church of his future See.

"This, from now on, is your name. No longer shall you be called 'the bishop'. This is a cloak that no longer fits the grand spirit that you are. Names do not denote just one's identity. Here, names speak to the laws of heaven to reveal your sacred truth that all may see."

He hadn't done so for many years. He couldn't even remember the last time he had shed a tear, even as a child. Yet now, here, knighted as he was with more than he could have best imagined, a tear found a course down his cheek.

"Your name, in the kingdom of heaven, dear Isaiah, is the key to open the higher levels of heaven's vast expanses. All who cross your path will know that your name is a true reflection of your innermost being. Whatsoever you do from here shall be written upon the records under your true name... Isaiah."

He tried his best, he really did! Yet he couldn't stop the tears from cascading down his face and onto his robe. But, as love would have it, Samuel's smile helped them both turn a solemn moment into the mirthful. Both started to laugh, easily at first, and then with a loosened restraint that resounded around the surrounding hills. Then, suddenly, Samuel's hand beckoned to silence. They both stopped to listen intently.

"Listen, my friend."

They stood, listening across the ethers, and to be sure, they both heard it. Their laughter seemed to echo in return through the hills and dales. Yet it was louder, much deeper and much louder.

He wasn't sure how much, or, if any time had passed since Samuel had taken his leave. Despite his lingering naivety about many things here in the heavenly realm, he knew that time was not a factor of control. There were no clocks or dials to signify the period. There was no night or day. No rotations of the sun by which to fix a quadrant. It was always perpetual light. Life seemed only to move between events. He could tell in detail of each of the experiences he had had so far. Yet he knew not the elapse of any time, nor its relationship to earthly measures. "I guess I'll find out soon enough," he said, turning to the elm tree that was his only current companion.

"Do you think the grand tree understands?" asked the silently approaching Elijah who was smiling at his friend's predicament.

"Oh, by the grace of God, Elijah. I have much to tell. I, I met, I mean, there was this beautiful soul. Samuel, he…"

"Yes, I know," said Elijah, clasping his friend by the arms with a hug of reacquaintance. "I am most pleased to make your acquaintance, Isaiah," he said with a mock bow that brought a smile to both their lips.

"Oh, stop it," said Isaiah. "You knew all the time, didn't you?"

"There is a long way between knowing something and the experience of it. But yes, I did play some small role in its unfoldment. Yet, there is still more to do."

"There is? What more of such array of surprises do you have lying in wait for me?"

Elijah said no more, merely moved forward to clasp Isaiah firmly around the waist.

"Are you ready to travel, my friend?"

A cursory glance spoke volumes of Isaiah's trust and love for his guide. The wise man inhaled deeply of the divine essence, then they were gone. At least, to Isaiah's proper senses, they were afloat. Together they sailed upward and through an atmosphere of both lightness and exquisite brightness. For Isaiah, they seemed to be moving into somewhere he could only describe as 'rarefied'. The very surrounds seemed to tingle with electricity as if moving through various layers of exalted ether. Although passing swiftly, he could discern scenes of the grandest, most far-reaching beauty that could not possibly be described in comparison to the human definition of same. Yet he was acutely aware that life's experiences had brought him to this point of wonder.

With his mind entranced by the fleeting moments of their passage, his distraction was brought to focus when he felt Elijah's strength start to wane. It was as if he could no longer rise in further coupling with his charge and, even with his depth of divinity, was drawing to the extent of his limits.

Then, they came to rest.

Standing before the pair was the most beautiful building that Isaiah had ever seen. He could not help it. He fell to his knees, hands clasped in benediction, before the grand object of his witness.

Chapter Ten

The Master

If only you could see what I see,
Glory upon glory to mine eyes.
Humbled before grace,
Mine eyes behold reflection of the most high.

Every word spoken,
An elixir to my ears.
Each smile beholden,
A balm to my soul.

By the grace, it is you!
My friend, our destinies entwined.
To serve our Father's children,
A purpose no grander could you find.

Wherever you go, take Me,
Said He.
Always together, separate we cannot be.
Only to ask and thou shalt receive.

I was still a little too stunned to assimilate that which had transpired across my journey. It seemed only moments before that I was entrapped within the constructs of my grief and raging sorrow. Now, I am here. I knew I would be eternally grateful to Atticus for bringing me to this place, but where my friend was at the given moment, I could not discern. I was still too captivated, not just by my surroundings, but the presence of the grand soul with whom I was speaking. Oh, my God! If you could only see what I, at that moment, beheld you would see the vast grandeur of ancient Rome or Greece at their pinnacle. The colonnades, the marble arches. Yet, this would do little to inspire your imagination to the spectacle of my current surroundings. He that sat before me in ease and recline and was in no way or by any resemblance an emperor or king. Yet, his demeanour was of itself enough to inspire an army of followers in his wake.

Young, in his prime, yet humbled by his grace of vast aeons of divine reason. His robe was white yet speckled with a rim of gold and blue brocade that was enough to highlight the depth of wisdom from his eyes, and love that exuded from each pore of his being. This soul, upon my previous enquiry, was the master of the wide dominion of our abode. He described his role as being to preside over a domain of heaven, yet I knew this was spoken humbly to moderate the vastness of his responsibility. Even so, I felt that his laughter and joyous camaraderie had made it seem as if I was his kin across the generations. We sat and spoke of many things, yet there seemed much more for him to add to my knowledge before he rose, moving toward the open portal looking out in expectation of further visitation. I was much too hesitant to ask of his expectation, despite the friendliness and ease of his welcome.

"Come, Athar, there is someone here to join us. I am sure you will be pleased."

He beckoned me to his side as we watched the two arrive side by side. One had full clasp around the waist of the other, much as Atticus had secured me on our journey here, before returning to his many duties. At the distance of their arrival, I could not make out the features of each. I could only notice the varied colours of their robes and discern their joyous abundance from the many and varied hues and shimmer of their attire. Perhaps it was the limited extent of my sight compared to the other, but I noticed, when approaching, one stopped suddenly upon seeing us both stand in await of their arrival. My supposition was that he was overawed by the majesty of the environment and buildings, just as I had been. Or perhaps it was the presence of the grand spirit who was master of the house, waiting to greet him.

But as my sight cleared and I saw who it was, I too was transfixed upon the spot, too stunned to even utter a word or express my surprise. Perhaps it was the touch of the master's hand to my shoulder or the dance of his glance of joy that was enough to break open my stupor. Whatever the case, I could no longer restrain my affection.

"Bishop," I yelled in advance of my catapult down the marble steps of his approach. So much in haste that I almost tripped over the leading edge of my robe, much to the mirth of the bishop's as yet unknown companion.

Our embrace as old friends long past but not forgotten was heartfelt for both of us. I could feel the warmth of his love through the clutch of his embrace as we hugged in mutual respect and recognition. When moved to arm's length, I could see the great change that had usurped his previous persona. It was a moment of great revelation to be reunited with he who had saved me from my torment. All previous thoughts of malice or revenge having been cast to a waste pile of detritus no longer required.

Watching on with a smile and knowing the depths of the hand of love upon the grace of the reunion, the Master summoned we three with an open gesture to join us in his grand sitting room.

Too overwhelmed to say much as we made our way up the steps and through the standing columns of alabaster and marble, we were invited to repose in comfort before the master's seat.

"It seems there is no need for an introduction to your friend, dear Athar," said the Master with a hint of mirth.

"Oh, no! By heaven's grace, I am so pleased to be reunited with my friend. Often I had cast thought to his current whereabouts and hoped for a joyous reunion."

"Oh, but you haven't heard the news, have you?" the Master

replied.

"News?" I said looking to the bishop in surprise.

"No longer is he addressed as such. Rather, he has earned the name which befits his standing within our heavenly realms. He is henceforth named as, Isaiah."

The bishop, I mean, Isaiah, smiled rather demurely at the pronouncement and I was most unrestrained in my effusiveness at the proclamation. I even promised most sincerely not to confuse the past with the present. I was then introduced to his friend and guide, Elijah, with whom I was most pleased to make acquaintance. Much time was spent in the retelling of past events that led us to the present moment, and tears of joy and laughter were shared each between the other, as we told of such happenings and experience. Then it was time for the Master to speak of the reason for our reunion in his halls of such benediction. We each of three fell silent before the Master's spoken word of revelation. At this point, Elijah moved away to further his duties elsewhere. It was only Isaiah and I left in the joyous company.

"Both you, Isaiah, and you, Athar, have traversed a road strewn with pain and suffering upon the earth and in heaven. Your paths have intertwined, then diverged, and now you once again stand upon the precipice of your interconnectedness."

I was only just able to remove my eyes from the depth of his gaze as he spoke to my soul, but I did manage to cast a glance towards Isaiah, who was as equally in thrall to every next word.

"Although separate of intent, both of you have divined a grand purpose to serve our Father's children in need, and for which you have my grand blessing – should you desire to fulfil it."

He paused for a moment to look to each of us with a gaze that seemed to explore our very depths. It was a moment of both inspiration and expectation. I knew, as did Isaiah, that this was a tipping point. We could be content with that which we had so far realised, or we could venture into what was yet to be known. We could stay fixed and satisfied with the road we had travelled, or we could be as the adventurer moving forward to the greater glory of exploration.

"Should you choose to remain as you are, know that our Father's love for you will be no less than the vast magnitude of what it is and always shall be. Fill your cups with His love. Should you seek further exploration, however, know that His divine hand will forever be found within your own."

I managed a peek towards my friend, Isaiah, and it was enough to see by his earnest demeanour that we agreed. It took no words, for we nodded our consent at the same moment, and the words that followed were the same, one for the other.

"When do we start?" we both said with burgeoning smiles.

The Master rose and beckoned us to follow.

"Come," he beckoned, "we should stroll in the garden. There is much we need to discuss."

He spoke with us of many things relevant to our journey whilst we strolled through his ornate garden of many florae. Much of which I have not yet the words of the earth to express in heavenly grandeur. Suffice to say that the multicoloured flowers were as none that I had ever before laid eyes upon. There was a rose so pure of essence that I could but gape upon its beauty and array of colours. All trees spoke of grace and filled the air with an essence of life not before seen nor observed. Even the grasses seemed to sing in harmony.

Imbued by the grace of the surroundings as we were, he spoke with us with words that gave us strength for that which lay before us. Yet, it was more than the words and the wisdom they contained. It was as if his words were filled with an elixir that so lifted our spirit. It was like being filled with an essence to supply our forward journey. Energy to not only traverse but to overcome. Glancing often at my friend, I knew well that he sensed the same and was now replete with a source of comfort and divine essence that would scale any mountain so presented before our fate.

Like much here in our heavenly abode, the moments in divine presence passed too swiftly to capture over time. It was when I espied Atticus and Elijah walking towards us that I knew our time in divine presence was now at an end, only to be replaced by the thoughts of its loving embrace. We, Isaiah and I, were ready. We knew what we were purposefully driven to achieve, yet we knew not the hills and dales we would climb in the realisation of such commitment.

Approaching with smiles at our reunion, both Atticus and Elijah, alive as they were to our charge, clasped us neatly to fold within the security of their embrace. Having acknowledged with heartfelt gratitude the grace with which we had been bestowed, we made transit back to whence we had come, in preparation for that which was to be.

Chapter Eleven

The Train Station

To what do I now bear witness?
A station? A crowd?
To what do they attend?
'Tis love that lies in wait.

Behold! It is I, your kin.
Grieve not, for I am here.
See you? It is me.
Our bond of love is alive.

Your time with me so precious,
My words soothing to thy spirit.
Here will I be,
Seek me and ye shall find.

Ask of me what you will,
I will guide you as I can.
Sleep, dear one,
For it is here that you will find me.

Isaiah and I took pleasure in the other's company. It was as if the recent experience with the Master had required us both to cast our spirit free upon the sands of restfulness. Not that we both felt in any way traumatised. Rather, it was as if we needed to assimilate the transformation. Sitting on the balcony of my abode as we were, we interspersed our recollections and conversations with giant pauses of, well, just sitting. It seemed to provide both the luxury of repose mixed with the elements of wonder and magnitude. We even took time to speculate about what we may achieve as we both evolved forward.

I was most eager to see my newfound knowledge used to its greatest effect for the many in need of its succour. Isaiah expressed the similar, but more to correct some of the errors and misdirection of religious and spiritual instruction for those with open ears. The reality was, however, that we were none the wiser as to how we could achieve such ends. I mean, to cross (back) over. To break open the veils between heaven and earth so that those with open hearts might hear. To cross the border and cast what we now know to be true to those in need was, for us, a grand undertaking. Yet one we knew not how to achieve.

"I guess when the moment is right, we will know what to do?" he said as I nodded my agreement. "Isn't that how it works? I mean, two eager disciples, as we are, will surely not be left to rest in repose as we attend future revelation."

It was right about that same moment that we saw her approaching through the garden. A stranger by regard, but not by a smile. A person unknown to both Isaiah and I, yet not without the bounty of love that preceded her introduction. Her mastery evidenced by the blue and yellow radiance festooned within the glimmer of her robe. When we saw the variant colours, we knew instantly that her being was filled with both the wisdom of truth and the grace of charity.

"May I join you?" she asked with an open-handed gesture that spoke of a joyous welcome of its own.

"By all means," I replied, as I positioned a chair such that she could join us in welcome communion on the balcony.

Both Isaiah and I rose in anticipation of greeting and thus had the opportunity to form first impressions of the delightful soul who joined our small gathering. Her flawless skin, though dark, seemed to radiate a lightness that bespoke the purity of her heart. Her eyes were like pools of obsidian that seemed to find no depths in their well. Yet, despite her grace, her dignity seemed only a reflection of her humility and compassion.

She required no need of our introduction for she spoke as if old friends; she told us that on earth, many centuries ago, she was known as Olivia, but that here, her 'nom d'heaven' was Cassiel. Pleasantries were cast forward and the grace of our Father's heaven was much discussed before she broke word to the purpose of her visitation.

"I come bearing the gift of your desire. I am sent as the Hierophant to further guide your education about the laws of heaven. Blessed knowledge that will serve you well on your quest to bridge the gulf between heaven and earth – for such cannot be used with malice or misdirection. It is only with the blessed touch of divine reason that this wisdom is freely given."

By glancing askance to quickly view the eagerness of my expression, Isaiah confirmed our earnest commitment to our task and implored her further elucidation of what we most needed to commence our journey.

"Come then, let us be away. There is much that I need to show you," she said standing to gently extort us to do the same.

Within but the fleeting moment of Cassiel's directive thought, we trio stood upon a small hilltop. The vista over which we laid collective eyes seemed but a short distance away, but far enough that we remained objective observers to the events as they unfolded. In amazement, what we saw impacted Isaiah so much that he could not restrain his exclamation of awe.

"By the grace of God," he exclaimed. "I have never witnessed such as that which now lays open before me. The closest I can relate my observations to, from my previous life experience, is that it is much akin to a train station of embarking and departing passengers."

"This analogy serves in close description to what is in effect happening," replied Cassiel.

"Look," I said pointing. "There, besides that grand oak tree. There seems such a great reunion between separated kin. A mother and child perhaps? And look! What are all those silver cords leading from many hearts that stretch across the ethers and over the mists?" There was so much going on that I could scarcely describe one scene without being distracted by another.

"Watch as their story is told and I will do my utmost to describe events for you," said Cassiel as we stood in silent amazement as the proceedings unfolded.

The mother, having hugged her son in a loving embrace, now moved to sit under the grand protection of the oak tree with her kin, whereby she commenced speaking in earnest to his open ears.

"What does she speak of?" I asked.

"Her son is much in need of guidance in his life and is sorely tempted to pursue a path that would not be in his eternal best interest. She seeks to instruct him in a manner that will secure him in the pursuit more fitting to his future progress."

Isaiah turned suddenly from his riveted attention to stare fixedly at Cassiel's declaration.

"But how? Is he not… dead and already passed to our abode here in heaven?"

Her smile of knowing did much to relieve both our pent-up inquisitiveness and increasing frustration.

"By no means. He will soon return to where he may, or may not, express the wisdom he has learned. The gift of free-will is forever writ as law upon the flesh."

"But how…?" I said in equal surprise to Isaiah.

"This, what you witness, is the meeting place. It is where those that sleep on earth can renew acquaintance with those kin with whom they are connected in love. Do you see those many silver cords attached to those many hearts? Do you see how they arc over the mists?"

Neither Isaiah nor I could respond, being struck by amazement as we were, but our collective nod was enough for our guide to proceed in explanation.

"These are visiting souls who, while in the depth of sleep,

can join loved ones upon their request. Their spirit is attached to their body through the silver cord that you witness. It is only when this silver cord is broken that their journey to heaven is considered 'one way', and they pass through the mists of judgement."

"Do you mean to say that all souls, when asleep, can connect with those they love?" I asked in earnest.

"Yes, of course. Love is the bridge, and as long as it remains strong and true, then one may call upon the other to guide and assist."

"But this is extraordinary," replied Isaiah. "If only such were known by many on earth. That one could connect with those we love beyond the veil. It would change much about how life is lived and in communion with those that have passed."

"Yes, it would. It is for this very reason that I have brought you here. To witness the magnificence of our Father's love for his children."

"Cassiel, do you mean to explain that the process of sleep whilst on earth is more than just a cause for the physical body to rest and recuperate from its travails," I hastened to inquire further.

"Oh, yes, much more. Think about it this way. When the human body rests, so does the mind. In such quietude, the spirit is free to explore the pathway between that which is on earth to that which is in heaven. No coercion or control is exercised; rather, the key is love and a heartfelt earnest desire to seek remedy and wisdom for life's burdens and hurdles that will enable the soul to bridge the veil by visitation."

"But how are they to know? How do they remember? How do they discern what is a dream and what is, well, real? If such connection is true, then much grief for loss would lessen in the knowledge."

"These are astute questions and observations, dear Athar. Let us, therefore, stroll amongst those that arrive. Perhaps then we can discern answers that as yet remain elusive."

Without further need for prompt or invitation, we each took the crook of the others' arms and made our way down the hillside, strolling amongst the throng of souls in various degrees of earnest conversation and/or embrace. As we strolled in grip of our wonderment, it was Isaiah who stopped suddenly in observation of someone standing alone and separate from others. The stretch of his silver cord evident, reaching back over the mists, and his stunned bewilderment to his surroundings most evident.

"Brother, Brother Isaac," cried Isaiah, as the startled visitor recognised the voice of attraction.

Isaac seemed so surprised at first that he could barely fall to his knees before his old friend without toppling over. "Bishop, I, I..." he stammered as he was lifted to his feet and embraced heartily by Isaiah. Turning to look at Cassiel, I could tell from her finger poised to her lips that she desired that I stay mute and in awe of the unfolding events.

"It is so good to see you, your Grace. You have been sorely missed by those that have mourned your passing. But how, I mean, where am I? I have not passed over myself, have I? I mean, I am not... dead? And what are these robes you wear? They are beautiful..."

Isaiah, through his kind look of compassion, was able to at least calm somewhat his friend's anxiety.

"No, my friend, you are not dead. It is not yet your time. Look! Do you see the beautiful silver cord attached to your heart that stretches back over the mists? You merely sleep but come seeking answers to some dilemma you face in your earthly abode. It is for us to determine what that problem is." As he spoke, Isaiah cast a hastened glance towards us as we watched in observation. It was a glance that at once told us that he was sure to his purpose but would call upon us if the need arose to a point of his impasse.

Isaac's frown did much to describe his inner turmoil as he at first struggled to articulate his conundrum. Then it was as if a dam broke open and the words came tumbling forth without restraint.

"Oh, my Bishop, my heart is sorely troubled. I can no longer hold to the rigid doctrines of our church and the expression of its sanctity. I have heard much in the thralls of confession that has so troubled my faith that I no longer know whether God's grace resides in my ability to minister His word. My lips have been sealed by the confessional, but my heart is rendered by holding its misdeeds within. In short, Bishop, I think I am losing my faith…"

Isaiah took firm hold of Isaac's shoulders and led him to repose under the welcome of a nearby elm that seemed to offer solace and support to the occasion.

"Isaac," he said as he sat next to his charge, "know that I am no longer your bishop, rather, that here, in heaven, I am known as Isaiah. I have been de-robed by the wonders I have both observed and experienced here within heaven's realm."

"But, by the grace of God, you were our bishop. How is that possible?"

"Fear not, my friend, the experiences by which I will now assist you have been sown by His divine hand. My eyes have been opened to the wonder of His laws of love, and which guide my voice to assist your suffering."

At once Isaac looked down at his chest and it was evident that his time at heaven's gate was shortening, for his silver cord became more vibrant and was tugging softly at his chest.

"Our time is short, my brother. Your human form reclaims its spiritual essence. Know therefore what is most important before you leave." Isaiah inhaled deeply before continuing and seemed to offer a silent prayer to He that held his hand. "Lose not your faith in God, my friend. The consequences to be borne by those that give scant regard to those precious souls under their care

are destined for harsh judgement in the halls of heaven. I know, I have been there. Follow the love in your heart. Treat all His children under the guidance of your care as if the children were your own. Protect and serve those that come to you for spiritual nourishment and NOT the bastions of the church that demand only fealty to its doctrines. I have seen much anguish here in heaven as caused by conformity to misguided orthodoxy and self-righteous obeisance."

At once, Isaac could withstand the calling no longer. The urge from his awakening body was much stronger in its beckoning.

"May I come again, my... I mean, Isaiah? Your words have been as a balm to my wounded spirit. Yet, I think there is much more I must learn."

Standing and waving farewell, Isaiah spoke truly, "By the grace of God, I will be here for you whenever you need me. I stand to no other law but the law of love. My heart will tell me when it is time for us to meet again. Go with God, my friend."

He watched with a gentle smile as Isaac felt the pull of the silver cord in beckoning to his return.

"Oh, oh, and one more thing," implored Isaiah as his friend started to drift away. "Never confuse chastity with purity. It is only the pure in heart who can see God." He watched as Isaac waved acknowledgement with a smile just as he was moving across the mists. Isaiah prayed it was enough.

Upon Isaac's departure, we moved together with smiles of gratitude and wonder, before again seeking answers from Cassiel. Questions that had started to form as a huge logjam in my burgeoning bag of unknowns. We strolled for a time, our silence filled with the surrounding chatter of conversations of the many souls and their companions, some in earnest, some in tears. But this time it was I who stopped suddenly in my tracks, only to have the others turn in surprise at my reticence.

"Cassiel, is it...? Would it be...? Could I...?"

"Speak your heart, dear Athar, and if it is within my power,

I will surely open my heart to your inquiry."

"My mother... Could I..." I managed to mumble further. "We were much estranged in my previous life. This is a burden I have carried for too long. Could I, I mean, is it possible for me to have visitation. To express now my, ah, forgiveness for that which has passed between us."

Cassiel thought deeply upon my request for a moment. It was a moment that seemed to evoke a flash of light transmitted to another sphere or a higher realm. Yet, in a moment, her answer was upon her lips.

"Yes, my dear friend, such a reunion is indeed possible. Yet, be aware that sometimes forgiveness is not readily received in the same spirit in which it is given. Sometimes the denial of responsibility is a stronger elixir than the evidence of truth."

I looked at her with an understanding that transcended my anxiety and nodded my confirmation, which she acknowledged with her eyes.

"Walk, then, over the hillside yonder," she said pointing in the direction. "It will be seen what your heart yearns to unfold."

Walking in the direction of her finger, my steps started to falter the closer I came to the crest over which I could not see. It was as if my heart was fixed strongly to its purpose, but my mind found falter the closer it came to its realisation. That's when I saw her. I knew it was her even though her back was turned to my presence. She could neither see nor hear my approach, but I knew it was her. The slant and slope of her taut shoulders and hands fixed firmly to her hips was something I recognised from many years of her overbearing presence.

"M, Moth, Mother," I croaked over vocals that did not wish to function without rasping over burning coals. "It is I."

"What, who, leave me alone," she said without turning, and with venom dripping from her tongue. "I don't know where I am, I have no wish to be here, and I certainly do not wish to speak with anyone. I want to return home. Leave me be."

Despite my being ill-at-ease, I took a further few paces forward in persistence.

"Mother, it is I, your son..."

Her quick turn to face me caused my abrupt halt fixedly in my tracks. Her face, full of the fire of malice, made her already stern visage even more difficult to admire in recollection. There were so few precious moments.

"I am glad you are here," I said, holding my hands forward to bridge the gulf between us. They were hands that remained empty of touch for she could only look at them as if they were foreign objects from an alien being.

"I just wanted to say, I mean, I sought this meeting to tell you that I forgive you. To tell you that despite the harshness of my life, the many trials that I endured by your neglect, I am happy. Here, now, in heaven, I am at peace with who I am. I came to thank you. For without you, I would not be in the exalted place in which I now abide. If it had not been for your self-centred intent, I would not be where I am at present. I could not have risen so high in God's holy order."

In the eternal moments after I had finished speaking and before she could utter a reply, I could but wonder where and why all those words just tumbled forward in presentation. My heart lay open in expectation of their gift of giving but quavered in fear as to what may be her reaction. I could not say that I was surprised, but I confess to a sense of disappointment in her response.

"Forgiveness? What are you forgiving me for? I did nothing wrong. I did what I thought best for you. I was your mother; you were my child – you were meant to obey me. That's how it works, isn't it! I stand no sense of regret for what I have done. My only disappointment is that I did not send you to that boarding school sooner. That way, I could have realised my true calling – without being hamstrung by the apron all that time. I mean, your father was never there, was he? Why don't you go to him with your forgiveness?"

I could barely keep my knees from buckling and struggled hard to hold fast to the truth about myself I had recently discovered. Yet somehow, I found the way to speak my heart before she was called back by the glare of her silver cord. "Go with God, Mother. He will be forever a light in your darkness. I stand steadfast in His glory but see that your eyes are closed to His brightness. I wish you could see what I see, but I fear your eternity will be a long one."

The urge from her silver cord was now one she could not refuse, and it was only her scowl that remained to pierce the darkness she had left behind after she flew back over the mists.

After she had gone, and as I strode back over the hill and across the vale with leaden feet, I was never so pleased to see my two friends awaiting my return with arms open.

Chapter Twelve

The Gatekeeper

If separation there be,
Between ye and Me.
Then love does not exist,
My gifts to you unworthy.

Return, you say, to right the wrongs,
Shine thy light for all to see.
Come, I beckon,
For more to see.

Guardian there be,
Can you not see?
Listen carefully, feel their touch.
Divine hands at your beckon.

Never absent shall they be,
At your behest, always.
Believe – ask and receive,
Seek and you shall find – let me show thee.

It was not long before we were able to move to another more serene, less frenetic location after the tumult of what had quaintly been nominated as the train station. It was a description that had rather tickled Cassiel's fancy because she kept referring to it as such, rather than its heavenly reference as the 'Abode of Reunion'. I know my friends did their utmost to revive my spirits after such a confrontation with my earthly mother. At the end of the day, however, I was satisfied that I had tried my best. I had spoken my truth and stood open to the response that may follow. I did confess to feeling rather depleted by the event, but at another level, I was happy to know that what was necessary had been done. I could neither facilitate the desired outcome nor alter what was not in my power to change. Pointedly, it was Isaiah who directed my thoughts to the inevitability of God's hand falling upon my mother's tortured soul and would, eventually, see her to the grace of His door for the love which awaits. I mused that it may not be me, but it would certainly be He that prised the light through her darkness, and that I would await such calling if it were my journey to pursue further intervention.

For the moment, we were content to amble amongst the delights of a hillside of forest that seemed to be alive with an incessant buzz of divine essence and flowers from trees of species I had long thought extinct from the abode of earth. It was like walking amongst a history book where that which had lived, still lives and flourishes under the guiding grace of eternity.

At the point of my feeling most sufficiently reinvigorated and ready to pursue whatever was so directed by the divine hand, it was Cassiel who opened my eyes to our next adventure of the spirit.

"I must leave you now, my gentle friends. But know that you are but a thought away from our reunion if I may be of service whenever you need," she said as she held us both within a loving embrace. "You will presently be visited by another who will assume your further instruction. You should find his depth of wisdom to be a boon to your expanse of learning. But for now, I bid you farewell." With this, she faded into the ethers of thought, a task that I confess still, to give me goosebumps as to how it is so possible to move hither and thither in such a space.

As Isaiah looked at me with one of those quaint smiles of his, I saw no better moment than to sit under the shade of a large forest specimen whose sweet berries seemed to play folly with the numerous birds flying about in travail. Isaiah joined me presently. But as love would have it, our repose was not extended beyond a few sweet moments of reflection before we were joined by the beautiful soul aforementioned by Cassiel. He introduced himself only as Adiel.

Bearing all the hallmarks of wisdom within his lithe frame, his face reflected an epoch amongst those of previous Middle-Eastern origin. Perhaps it was the lustre of his skin or the reflection of love, wisdom and grace in his eyes, but whatever the case, it required no further judgement to behold another messenger from whom we were to be inspired along our journey. As I watched, I could not help but wonder how amongst so many souls resident in heaven and on earth, each one felt the touch of God's hand as ever-present when need so demanded His presence.

"If ever there was a separation between the divine and His children, then God's love would not exist," Adiel said in response to my thoughts as if they were spoken out loud. "May I join you in repose? It seems such a place that the soul can learn to enjoy the sum of its glory."

"Be at home, my friend," replied Isaiah. "You are most welcome, and I surmise you to be the gift that was so warmly previewed by Cassiel's careful attention to our needs."

"I am such as directed, and stand ready to avail of my services as they may project you forward on your mutual quest, my brothers. But may I suggest we stroll amongst the surrounding hillsides? I find the vista of God's wonder to be a source of constant inspiration to the words that will flow between us."

No further prompt was required as we aimed to nowhere particular, being rather content to be one with the other in profound discourse, and similar admiration of the majesty of colours and essences that the amassed flora availed at its liberty.

"I am to understand, dear Isaiah, that your wish is to seek to correct many of the untruths about heaven that pervade so many of the earth's systems of beliefs, is that not so?"

"It is most certainly, my brother. I am most sorely vexed at many of the doctrines that simply do not adequately describe the majesty of that of which I am now aware. Much that I know now would provide liberation to many souls, if known to those now shackled within the binds of misdirection and falsehood."

"A worthy quest, indeed. And you, dear Athar," he said, turning to me with eyes that spoke more love than his words could reveal. "You have expressed the desire to care for those in suffering and grief. This also is an aspiration worthy of a hero's errand."

I was well aware that I knew but a fragment of the expanse of God's blessings in heaven, but after Adiel's praise, I was certain that one could still blush when I felt my face flow with heated radiance.

We continued to stroll at ease and silence for a short while. Even without the anticipation of an expected destination, I was reasonably certain that a divine hand was moving us towards the desired point of our next exploration... and so it proved to be.

"Ah, look, over yonder," said Adiel pointing. "I do believe that is a convenient destination for your progress. Perhaps we should pay a visit. There is much that I believe can be learnt within its hallowed halls."

The building we approached seemed to be, from the outside anyway, much like many of the hallowed buildings that we had by grace seen previously on our travels. Yet, this one appeared different in a way that I had yet to assimilate. I mean, the construct seemed the same. The stately columns, the opulent gardens in which we strolled had many souls in course of communication, reading, or just musing along a line of thought. Turning to look at Isaiah, I could see from his frown and the tilt of his head, that he too was in a similar conundrum. There was something different, but neither of us could place its difference.

Adiel stood not much on ceremony as he entered the rather large ornate doors and, beckoning us forward, moved into the large area of reception where his presence was exalted by many who gave blessings for his arrival. He seemed like an old friend to many and was acknowledged with hands held to heart or namaste.

Before I could voice question as to our proper location, he urged us forward into what he described as the main hall of lecture. It was a room structured as an auditorium that held many eager students in the thralls of a class of instruction. We were invited to take a seat amongst the many, as Adiel moved to stand by the teacher in midst of her lesson.

"Adiel, we are most blessed by your presence. I see that you have brought us two new, eager learners. I will stand aside to allow you to speak to the assembled, as the depth of your wisdom far exceeds the limitations of my own."

"Let it not be so. I am certain that where you stand with the lesson is the perfect place for our two new learners to expand upon their knowledge." Having spoken, Adiel moved to the side of the room and sought only to offer the grace of his presence, and space for the teacher to proceed.

"Students," she said pointing to the illustrations on the board behind her. "Your role as spirit guides is one of the most cherished by our Father. It is one critically important for those that assume an earthly body and who seek to further their evolution in the scheme of God's holy empire."

As she paused momentarily, I just managed to sneak a glance towards Isaiah who was as equally rapt to attention as I was. Both of us keen to hear the next and ongoing part of the discourse.

"As you are aware, you will be assigned a special soul to tend as that soul pursues the purpose of their life on earth. You have been specially assigned to such a task, by reason of the love you hold in your heart and the assimilation of your knowledge that best assigns to that soul's advancement. The hand of God binds the union, and your job is to help and care for them in any way that you positively can."

At once, one of the hands of an eager student raised forth to ask a question and was acknowledged to speak by the teacher.

"But many on earth are not gifted with the ears to hear. Many do not listen even if properly instructed. Many are taken to temptation away from their divine and designated purpose. What then are we to do when our words fall to deaf ears and onto blind hearts?"

"You indeed speak the truth. Yet, as a spirit guide, you must leave expectation behind and stay mindful of the spark of love inherent within all. Seek always to break down human ignorance respecting natural law. This is the pathway to truth. It will not serve your guardian's soul should you fall to despair about their lack of progress or descent into the vortices of temptation. Remain always to hand and by their side, wherever and whenever they should have need. There will be a time when they will call upon you. When they have so reached the nadir of impasse or despair. Or, when the spectre of death falls like a shadow of grief over their life. Then will be the time to cast your wisdom upon their ear, or your urgings to guide them to the gateway of redemption. This will be the time when you, the gatekeepers of precious souls, will be forever blessed by such service to His children."

She then turned toward the by-standing, Adiel. "Adiel, perhaps you would like to add further to the present discussion. You are, after all, the most adept of we the gatekeepers. Your aeons of experience would much avail to the well of inspiration for these students."

He stepped forward to the centre of attention, but by no means showed any sign of self-importance toward the adulation he received. Each pore of his being radiated a humility belying his depth of wisdom.

"It is true, over the aeons, I have been spirit guide to many in earthly form. I have learned much to support your well-being in such regard." Looking directly at me, he motioned gently that I should come to join him before the class.

"Athar, would you please join me?" he said gesturing by his side. It was an invitation I could hardly refuse.

"My dear, Athar, do you remember, when you were in human form, to a time when you were most beset by trouble."

"I do remember such," I replied with a hint of reservation, not wanting to dig into such past as I had recently transformed, but not forgotten. I knew, however, that I was in good hands and would not be cast adrift.

"Do you recall times when you were in despair but felt that slight touch, or chill to your neck or spine? When you saw no one around, and there were no other means, but you felt someone beside you?"

I thought for a moment, then came to excitation by my recollection. "Yes, yes, I do remember. There was a time when I was in such torment. Alone and bereft of a friend, but then was the time I recall someone stroking my hand. It was as if they were trying to tell me something or ease my distress. I remember now! I could almost hear the words. It was like, 'You are loved...' or 'I am here...' but I couldn't quite hear. I was too afraid."

"Yes, and now you know that that was your guardian angel speaking with you, do you not?"

"Wow," I said in wonder – a response that drew some small titters of laughter from the group.

"Do you recall another time, when you felt such an urge in your being – I believe on earth, it is crudely referred to as, 'gut feel' – to go somewhere or do something to save you from imminent trouble?"

"Yes, again, indeed I do."

"Well, my friend, that indeed was your spirit angel imploring you with the urgency of advice. Advice essential for your well-being, safety, even."

This time it was I who turned to the students and held out my hands to orchestrate the proper reaction.

"Wow!" they all expressed in a chorale. Followed by much laughter and joyousness.

"Thank you," said Adiel with a smile. "You had better return to your seat before the whole class turns to an uproar." I did so with haste, but even Adiel could not stop the round of applause I received with a slight bow.

"Now, students," said Adiel resuming control of proceedings. "I would call such as this a 'pivot point' with your charge. As you know, your guidance can be given at any time. It does not take a crisis or problems to exert such influence. I urge you at times such as these to persist in your efforts, to speak with divine reason in the good times, and more so in the dolorous. Maybe, just maybe, your guidance will become relied upon at ALL times. Have faith, my brothers and sisters, that your work is not, and never will be in vain."

At that very moment, I happened to look towards Isaiah, knowing as I did those previous doctrines of his learning spoke about communications with so-called spirit guides, such as these, as being 'from the devil'. I was most pleased, but not surprised when I watched him rise from his seat and start to clap. At first a little hesitantly, but then with great vigour. Indeed, his enthusiasm was contagious, because he started a crescendo of clapping amongst the cohort of many other open ears.

Later, as we reposed under the awnings of a large pagoda, both Isaiah and I took the opportunity to delve further into that which we had just witnessed. It was a discussion that took more effort than normally considered. Adiel's concentration was frequently interrupted by many passing students offering appreciation or seeking further words of advice for their challenges ahead.

"It has been a great day of instruction, for which I thank you deeply," said Isaiah when the last of the students had returned to their classes. "I understand that I am at once full to the brim of new truths and expanded knowledge. Yet, I know not how much remains to learn, nor whether we are both ready for the experiences that lie ahead."

Inhaling deeply, Adiel looked at us one to the other, as if making an assessment or judgement of a forthcoming action.

"Would you like to experience that which we have readily spoken of? Would you care to see how directly we of the spirit world can communicate with our brethren on earth when the channels are opened by love and, more importantly, through the absence of fear?"

I looked at Isaiah at the same moment that he looked at me. It was like osmosis. We were as kin and able to assimilate the other's thoughts without bias or misinterpretation. We both nodded eagerly in anticipation.

Holding his hand up by way of caution, Adiel added, "I ask as we journey together that you remain in observation only. I would not wish to overwhelm my charge with burdens of excess. Rather, I will seek only to demonstrate the facility and ease of our transaction when so availed by the purity of the soul with whom we commune." To this declaration, we again nodded our assent.

"Good, then let us to the task."

Standing in the middle and taking both myself and Isaiah firmly around each waist, we seemed to be transported at the behest of Adiel's thought. It was like flying through mists. I could feel at once the sensation of his grasp firmly to embrace my heart, so I knew that I, and my colleague, Isaiah, were not cast out without the prospect of return. I knew that neither he nor I held any over-compelling attachment to earth, binding us in thrall to its memories. I knew therefore without asking that we were not to be left in the purgatory between heaven's

122

door and the portal of earth. In short, I knew we were secure in Adiel's safe hands, and that love would hold sway upon any other sense of foreboding.

As the mists cleared and my already acute senses were becoming attuned to the more harsh and lower vibrations of the earth's abode, I found myself in a room along with my two colleagues. And then there was another. I could see her, and I could feel the gentleness of her spirit even before she spoke. The study room in which she was seated at her desk, working on her computer, was not one of overwork or disorganisation. Rather, everything in her environment seemed to be at peace with itself and communal to a sense of calm presence. By my calculations, she appeared of early-middle age with the first signs of grey peeping through her lush auburn locks. Her smile as she turned, even before the announcement of our presence, was like filling the room full of sunshine.

"Adiel, is that you?" she sparked at the sense of his presence.

"Yes, dear one, it is I."

"I am honoured by your visit. Have you a message to impart? Do I need instruction to push me from errant tasks?"

"Oh, no, my dear Julie. You are most blessed in the eyes of God. Your works of service to His children are a boon in a sea of turbulence. Your presence strikes a chord of joy wherever and whomever you pass by on earth's journey."

"Adiel, do I sense others' presence with you? Are you not alone?"

"You are a gifted spirit, indeed, dear friend. Yes, I have brought two colleagues with me, if I may be so bold to their introduction."

"If it is your will, Adiel, then I am at your service in any way I can help."

"Thank you. I have brought with me the presence of both Isaiah and Athar to show them how easy may be the facility to commune with those on earth. How we in spirit can cross the bridge if only the love is strong and true."

"My heart warms to their presence, dear friend. I can feel their love shine through their eagerness to ask a barrage of questions. But I fear that your instruction will be so much the better than mine will ever be," she said, turning to look at both Isaiah and I, without really being able to see the form, but knowing of our presence through the sense of feeling.

"I am most glad of your invitation. Indeed, I have asked my colleagues to stay mute so as not overawe the occasion. Although, if I may, could you please tell them how, in your case, it is possible to openly commune with us in the spirit form."

"I would be most pleased, dear Adiel. This is a discourse I have had with many, but with few who have ears to hear." She paused slightly, inhaled deeply, and seemed to draw from a well replete and full of inner inspiration. "My friends, since I was a child, I knew that I was blessed by the presence of spirit. As a child, I remember seeing and hearing things that I knew were sent from my guardian angels. These guiding hands have never left me, despite many attempts at strangulation of these gifts by my parents, peers and their doctrines forced upon me. I have never turned aside from these blessings, much to the angst of those who believe these gifts to be the device of the devil. I could no more remove my sense of love for these bestowed blessings than I could sever my hand from my arm."

"You have spoken wisely, dear Julie, and I thank you for your openness of heart in such regard," replied Adiel.

"I am the one who has been blessed, dear friend. Please avail your friends to ask of me should they need my assistance as their journey progresses."

"We take our leave until next time, then. And, as you know, you have but to call and my assistance will be freely given to your needs. Blessings, my friend."

As we took our leave, I watched as Julie returned unperturbed to her work on the computer. The only evidence of our presence

I could discern was the slight smile on her face and the thought she held to her position before the interruption by our presence.

When we returned, it was to our spot under the same tree where both Isaiah and I had reposed when first met by Adiel. This time, however, it was without Adiel's pleasant company. He had left us with the words that he would attend to our needs within coming events. But that, for now, we were best served in repose to allow all that had preceded to integrate to the proper foundation within our respective spirits.

Neither Isaiah nor I needed any further prompting in such regard...

Chapter Thirteen

The Returning

Darkest memories know thee,
Face the truth of it, you must.
Fear not, My hand is in thine,
Together, united we face this demon.

Passageway leads to hell's gate,
Forbode and terror surrounds.
Make it I cannot, fear grips me,
Yes, you can, I am here.

Begone, I have no need of thee,
Leave me to my torment.
My terrible sins, shackle me,
I beseech thee, leave me be.

Nay, this I cannot do,
Forgiveness is mine to give.
Unburden thy soul,
Tarry not, follow me.

It wasn't so much that I required rest, it was just that the sheer expanse of events as they had unfolded played as a cinematic screen across the extent of my thoughts. I turned to Isaiah, who was as I, reclining against the trunk of a sprawling willow. It must be said that the gigantic edifice was doing its level best to reinfuse its two cohabitants with renewed vigour. It was entirely possible to feel the overt transfer of the divine essence which flowed from its broad torso and fragrant blooms.

I'm not sure how long Isaiah and I remained in such a state.

I had previously confessed to my friend how I was still much perplexed about the passage of time here in our heavenly abode. Isaiah did his best in explanation by telling me that time, in this new life, seemed to be measured by results achieved, and not by any revolutions of the sun, of which there was none – it was ever perpetual, well, light.

"Athar," said Isaiah, turning to me with that furrowed brow I had come to know so well. "I think there is something we have missed. Something that we have both overlooked in our quest to pursue our stated objectives."

Knowing him as I now did, I looked at him curiously without quite being able to pierce the depths of his concern.

"I fear in bringing forth this subject; it is not my wish to break open old wounds that may as yet be insufficiently healed. My love and concern for you have grown to such extent that I could not bear to see you further pain."

I watched my friend closely as his face reflected the depth of his feelings through his words. I took much comfort in knowing that I now have a companion, forged as it were through a cauldron of fire, yet now exalted in the eyes of He that ministers to our hearts without guile or mischance.

"Speak your heart, my friend. If the cause is righteous, then together we can surmount any perceived obstacle within our path. What is it that troubles you so?"

I watched as he took a large intake of the air of divine elixir and started searching for the words to begin.

"When both you and I were in earthly form, you as barely a child and I as the then bishop of my See, there was one who vexed our lives most severely. In the great paradox, it was he who through his abhorrent behaviour, has now brought us together as kindred spirits, yet whose actions have caused us both much pain."

I knew in an instant who he was referring to. Brother Ignatius was his name, and as he was recalled, so did a clump of bile rise in my chest. It was still so difficult to remember his face without bearing the pain of his deeds. For more than a few moments, I could not find a voice for the turmoil of my thoughts. Even when Isaiah reached for my hand, I could feel a cold shiver steer a course through my being like a blade.

"I, I do not, I cannot..." I managed only to stammer.

"Yes, I know, dear Athar. I too am much complexed by such regurgitation of the past. Yet, something gnaws at my soul that remains a cross to bear."

I saw such a depth of sorrow and concern in my friend's eyes that it was almost enough to drag me from my stupor.

"Why? I mean, I understand. I, like you, have felt his presence here in heaven as a spirit. I know he has passed to the nether regions, yet I have not had courage enough to open the door to its proclamation."

"Yet," he said in reply, "given all that we now know, all that we have seen and experienced by the grace of our Father, is it not time to reclaim our torment? How can we, knowing so much as we now do, stay mute to his suffering? Even for all that he has caused us to endure. If we, exalted and blessed as we are, cannot minister to whom we have known as most vile, surely then our evolution remains bound to his rock without wings to fly."

I well understood his meaning and struggled hard to find a grasp of his words that would shake me to move according to their higher purpose. I confess that it did take eternal moments before I struggled to my feet to stand before my cherished friend as he sat staring up towards me.

"We will do it! You and I! We will do what is, by the grace of God, our highest calling. Yet should we fail in such pursuit, it will be with the force of God's love in our right hand and His staff of light in our left. Let us be to our task, good friend. And let us pray that we can secure our brother's soul from the midst of his purgatory."

The passageway was dark. As dark as I could yet explain without delving into the occult. It was as if malignant spirits stood sentinel before every step we took in advance. Voices of menace spoke loud to our ears and seemed determined to sway our intent to proceed. The cavern through which we traversed would, to many, appear too far removed from the benign to continue. It was as much by the feel of hand as the luminous light of our robes that we proceeded through the miasma. Oft-times, more than once, either Isaiah's strength seemed to wane in pursuit of our destination, or then it was mine that succumbed to the depths of despair inherent in our journey through this passage of deepest purgatory. Most fortunate it was that we had each other to fortify our waning reservoirs of strength as we stepped forward with determination.

"This is a horrible place," I said breathlessly to my companion. "If this is an eternal rest, then woe betide he that undertakes such pursuits on the earthly plane. If eternity's door cannot be opened, then I fear those who are captured within will see darkness and malice as their only friend."

"Yet, we have been led here by the grace of His hand and stand ready to face whatever the darkness shall nigh reveal," said Isaiah as breathlessly as I.

At once there was a sound, a kind of rustle, that spoke of a presence in the near distance. I tried to pierce the darkness with my sight but could barely see the hand placed before me. Then there was the scream. A hideous scream, so loud that it made tremble the very bones of my essence.

"Who goes there? Who are you? Whoever you are, do not come closer. I despise your very presence. Leave now and forever depart. I have no wish for whatever you offer."

I felt the very core of my being sway before this malignancy, and I held out my hand to clasp severely upon Isaiah's arm to warn him of any further approach. With strength I knew that I did not yet possess, Isaiah placed his hand upon mine as if to reassure me of his fortitude. It was a strength that I had not before witnessed and was comforted by its touch. It was enough for us to take some further tentative steps forward, despite the invocation of pending doom.

"We come not to harm, friend. We merely wish to make ourselves known to your presence," said Isaiah, in a voice that held fast to the strength of comfort.

"I do not need such introductions. I am safe here and have no wish to open the door to any who would do me harm or who would cast me into the fire which awaits my earthly deeds."

"There is no need for concern in such regard. We are here only to speak with the tone of forgiveness. Your deeds stand before you yet unrequited, but we stand steadfast by the grace of His hand to offer you such forgiveness that will release you from these bonds of darkness."

There was a pause, and a shuffling about as if he were set in motion to try to remove himself from his current station but could find no other means of release from his servitude. Finally, he stood fast and peered at us through the darkness, with eyes reddened by the fatigue of sentry.

"Who are you to offer forgiveness? I seek not your forbearance for that which I have done. I can no more deny my deeds than I can expunge them from memory. I am resigned to my fate and have no wish to claim anyone's forgiveness for my sins. Go from here, you both, and trouble me no more with your pious renditions."

I do not know where it came from, nor do I even know what prompted me to step forward, yet I could no more resist the impulse than I could deny my feet moving forward. At that moment my robe seemed to come alight with an essence I never before knew existed. It seemed to shine across my face to pierce the gloom so that I could be seen in fullness.

"Do you not know me, Brother Ignatius? Do you not see the reflection of the child within the face of the prime man before you?"

The echo of silence through the darkness of the chamber passed like an eternity before I heard his sharp intake of breath, with the knowledge that he recognised the child who stood before him.

"You, I, it cannot be true..." he stammered, trying to find words that described the vortex of his inner torment. "Why are you here? I did, I mean, I caused you..."

"Yes, you did! It is true! In the past, my hand was raised to smite your very being and curse you to the known ends of the world. Yet, here I stand, ready to offer my hand to your redemption, should you so desire it."

Seeing the extent of my effort to remain centred on my purpose, Isaiah strode readily to my side to offer his support and relief.

"And I, Brother, do you not recognise me?" he said stepping into the vague light.

"B, Bish, Bishop, truly it is you," the stricken man stammered. "How is it that you are here? My thoughts lay open to my deceit and stand mute before the tacit truth that the church availed my impoverished actions through silence. I stand condemned before your presence now so overt."

"I come neither to condone or condemn your actions. Nor will I emote the extent of my soul's torment for my insouciant hands and denial of the truth. I come only to offer you the hand of passage to take you from this pitiful existence to guide you towards the light of God's grace. He that stands ready to offer you a passage from this darkness. Both Athar and I offer you the light to see you from this cesspit of your creation."

I could freely feel the tremble course through his feeble soul at the strength of Isaiah's words. It was as if he were caught between the fear of redemption and the pleasure of captivity.

"Wh, wh, where would you take me? I, I have much to endure in recompense for my sins. I fear greatly the hand bearing the sword of revenge for the horrors that I have committed."

Again, I am not sure where it came from, nor how the words found the proper course to my voice, but I could not deny them from pouring forth. "Fear not for I am with you. I take not your hand in revenge, but to deliver you from the evil of your creation. You are never alone, and the pain you will endure is not suffering, rather, the light of My Hand to guide you forward."

It didn't take so long to exit as it did to enter, despite the hesitancy of his leaden footsteps. There seemed to be a soft light shining on our pathway to deliver us from this den of iniquity. Isaiah and I spoke only in need to offer support as we led Ignatius from his cavern of despair. Even the attendance of a messenger waiting upon our exit from the darkened portal was dressed such as not to overwhelm our charge with the force of blinding light. Rather, his gentle touch and explanation as to his purpose noted to guide Ignatius' future security. It was all we needed to know that our travails were now tended by the love of our Creator's hand.

We watched silently as Ignatius was led away by an awaiting comforting hand to a further destination, perhaps not in peace, but most assuredly in love. Seeing them fade into the distance I turned to Isaiah and could instantly read his thoughts and lopsided smile. We were to return to the surety of the awaiting willow that had so graciously before secured our repose. We couldn't wait to get back.

Chapter Fourteen

The Recovery

A tale to chill the soul, told she,
Life's blossom curtailed.
Misguided truth, abhorrent deeds.
Eternal burdens await.

My son, my son, they took him from me.
Cursed art thou,
Hate thee, do I,
My heart burns, lost.

My son, my son,
I finally found thee.
My dying eyes, my last breath,
I embrace thee.

Rest now, sweet soul,
Unburden thy heart.
Cleanse the malice from your being,
Let the light claim thee.

It really should not have come as a surprise to find both Atticus and Elijah standing comfortably in attendance when Isaiah and I found ourselves, by the speed of our thoughts, back to the weeping willow. The passage of time most certainly had no meaning when embraced by my colleagues in the joy of reunion. Nor had separation diminished in any way the heartfelt camaraderie between us. Indeed, I guessed that neither Atticus nor Elijah required an encyclopaedic rendition of all that we had just traversed, but they were content to listen as Isaiah and

I poured forth the contents of our hearts in an expression of the wonder of our most recent journey.

Sometime during our rather one-sided discourse, I noticed how Elijah cast a glance with a smile across to Atticus. I couldn't help but truncate Isaiah's monologue with a pert question.

"What? What's the matter? Have we said something funny?"

"Oh, no, dear Athar, but you haven't noticed," said Atticus with a beam.

"Noticed? Noticed what?"

"Look," said Elijah pointing at our robes.

I looked across to the perplexed Isaiah at the same moment he looked at me... and there it was... our robes, they had changed colour. It was as if they had been washed and cleansed. No longer was there any trace of darkness or abhorrent malignancy. They were radiant. The colours were more vibrant than any I could begin to reimagine on earth. It was as if the colours of a rainbow had been infused with luminous light.

"Well, I'll be..." said Isaiah as he smoothed over the folds with the palms of his hand. "My friend," he said, gently slapping his hand to my shoulder and trying to suppress his laughter, "it looks as if we've been taken to the cleaners."

Laughter resided amongst us and played merrily with our proper senses until it was again time to press upon more important matters. Led by Elijah in his usual staccato manner as he stood erect and peered over the hills into the far distance.

"Come," he said, "it is time for your next feast of knowledge. You need to meet someone."

The small house seemed rather plain, nondescript, even. Yet, from the outside, it appeared neat and tidy with all the necessary rudiments for a quaint abode occasioning enough room to accommodate a sole occupant. The garden was arrayed with small boxes of flowers in the early stage of bloom, and the growth of trees seemed to be as fledgelings to the monoliths to which we had grown accustomed. As we approached, the resident could be seen in the repose of a garden chair, sitting overlooking the beauty of the surrounding hillside. It was a scene, despite its lack of comparative grandeur, that seemed to place the observer in a position of relative peace.

The person's reveries were interrupted by Atticus' call of arrival, and she turned her expression into a smile as both Elijah and Atticus moved ahead to embrace her open arms with the gift of a happy reunion.

"Oh, I am so happy to see you both," she said. "It has been too long in the offing that I have not been graced by your presence."

As the pleasant scene unfolded, I was able to gain an impression of her demeanour as both Isaiah and I awaited a proper introduction. Her dark hair flowed as a cascade beyond her shoulders, and to estimate in earthly terms her age would be to say she was nearing upon the prime of womanhood. Her robe, whilst not radiant nor multi-hued, seemed to possess the potential for emerging colours, but as yet had not found their reason to bloom.

Lagging slightly behind as we approached, Isaiah looked to me with those crossed brows as he does. "I know this young woman. I have seen her before, but I cannot now place it to the present." At that very moment, we were with them.

"My dear Mary," spoke Atticus, "we have brought with us two colleagues with whom we are sure you will find kinship. Athar and Isaiah have journeyed far together and have been set to purpose for God's higher calling. Could we avail upon your graces to tell your story to these fine souls? They, I am sure, will be further enriched by your history that will serve them for the trials ahead."

"You have but to ask, dear Atticus," she replied, but then seemed to hesitate for a reason known only to her. "But I fear that my story may be overburdened with scant reserves of strength in the telling. I would not wish your friends to think ill of me if I am unable to fulfil the fullness of your expectations."

"Fear not, Mary," spoke Elijah with a comforting hand to her shoulder. "We are both here to ensure that as much as they are benefitted by your story, you too will be enriched by its telling. We are as close to you as a teardrop to an eye."

"I am much comforted, then. Let us to seats and first begin with admiration of our scenic view across the hillside. Thus, we will start with delight at the beginning as my story unfolds." And so, her story began...

"I was born and raised to a community that by its very definition precluded many others. The foundational cornerstones of belief and doctrine provided not just a ladder which to scale, but also a barrier fence through which only the selected and strictly pious and devoted could enter. By the age of four, I was habituated to dress in a manner appropriate to my age and gender. I was structured within a pattern that included strict adherence to the rules as proclaimed by the elders of the community, whose very utterances were declarations to the holy word. Severe penalties were applied upon disregard of these rules, and it was more than once that I felt the sting of my father's cane upon my bare buttocks as a penalty for infractions that I now do not recall."

"By the age of ten, I was both flower-girl and housekeeper in assistance to my mother's chores and my seven siblings across various ages. I was taught the deemed proper place for a woman and was instructed in the functions that defined my role via gender. I was not by any stretch of my imagination a naughty girl, but the welts oft received at some perceived slight or infraction gave me cause to harbour malice and anger towards he who took pleasure in the infliction. But I was good at hiding. During daylight hours, I was ever the smiling, obedient child. My automatic response of, 'Yes, Father, no, Father,' was most usually followed by my demure look to the floor upon which I stood before his hulking frame."

"As the years bloomed, so did my body and I became

accustomed to the errant stares towards my developing frame. It was not uncommon that I felt the glancing touch or brief stolen caress as I passed by members of the community, young and old, as we moved close in a crowded aisle or passageway. Those turbulent teenage years only seemed to overflow my nightly hours with thoughts of malice and harm to those who so confined my burgeoning spirit. Notwithstanding, I was still the ever-devoted child at our Sunday service, and I was always the one to hold the younger ones in thrall during Sunday school. Little did they know that my heart was a cauldron that despised their words and pious renditions of proclamation. It was hard to smile when they told me it was 'God's will' when they were at liberty to exercise their ogling eyes, errant passion, and fierce control under the auspices of His holy name."

"I imagine it comes not as a surprise to tell you that by the time of my eighteenth birthday, I became pregnant to a young boy's chance encounter. He was handsome, gallant, and external to our community. By definition, he was an 'untouchable'. He was a sinner and 'of the devil' for his denial of the true faith. Perchance, he had no faith at all. But his touch was as golden silk upon my trembling skin. I could no more resist his passion than I could deny my own. To this very day, whatever happened to the boy upon discovery of my condition, I do not know. All I know is that he disappeared, never to be seen again. His fate is unknown to me. My fate and the hardships that followed, however, were yet to be revealed."

"In short, despite my endless protestations, entreats and appeals to their decency, my baby was taken from me at birth. I was told that it had not survived the passage, but I knew this was a lie. They took my baby from me, and it was not until many years later that I was able to find him again as an adult."

"I hated them! I detested them all. Their pious murmurs, their self-righteous piety. I rebelled. I became an uncontrollable rage to their sanctimonious indignation. I would not leave the home except in an attempt to flee. I railed against their every wish and was more than once pronounced to be 'filled with the devil'. They even tried to exorcise its presence from my condition. Yet nothing they did was resolved to their satisfaction. I could no more bow to their wishes than I could release my demons of self-destruction. Eventually, I escaped."

"The streets became my home, and my only solace was found in the bottom of a bottle or the freedom I pumped into my arm. Once, at the depth of my despair, I was found and taken to a nearby hospice to secure my relief. It worked for a while, but my demons were stronger and for many years hence I was cast amongst the vagabond. The only thing holding my life together was the feeble thought of reunion with my child."

"My sole saving grace was that upon my dying breath, my son managed to find me. He too was so driven to my discovery that it had consumed his life for many years. Our tears of relief upon our reunion were all that helped my passage to where my spirit now abides. I repose gratefully in the knowledge that my son's love remains fixed to my heart. Yet, I came to heaven's door a soul twisted by the maltreatment of others and the curse of revenge upon my lips that has thus far polluted the very reaches of my being."

It was evident from her lengthy descriptions that her spirit was flagging. The telling of her story had so depleted her reserves that Isaiah and I became concerned for her well-being. At this same moment, both Elijah and Atticus came to her side to offer support and comfort. She was taken to rest by caring hands. Elijah remained to care for her needs, whilst Atticus rejoined us to commune of the experience.

Overawed somewhat, as we both were, Atticus allowed precious moments to pass without speaking as we gazed fixedly across the hilly expanse. We felt no small measure of heaven's grace to reinfuse our somewhat depleted reserves. Eventually, it was Isaiah who broke open the seal of quietude with an exclamation of his discovery.

"I know now! I know where I have seen her before. It all makes sense," he said, turning to Atticus. "She was at the chorale, wasn't she? She was one, along with Athar, who was ministered so profoundly by the hand of grace. The magnetic light! In the auditorium…"

Atticus' smile beamed brightly as Isaiah correctly recalled the event.

"But how? Why? How is it that she still labours? I recall her exit from the magnetic chorale as one of grand majesty. Her crippled body was renewed, was it not? She was released from her bonds."

"Your eyes did not deceive you, good Isaiah, but they did see only that which was sorely imposed upon her spirit by others, not the consequences she incurred upon herself."

"Huh? I don't understand," he replied, his furrowed brow deepening more than ever before.

"The wonder of the magnetic chorale is, as you rightly say, a miracle of God's breeze upon the afflicted. Yet, its reparations pertain only to those which others have caused to the deformity. In Mary's instance, her spirit was denied and deformed by the errant hands of doctrine that in no way resembles our Father's true teachings. Her father was the bearer of the scythe that smote her sweet blossom. She was like the budding flower, and he the one who poisoned the growth of her roots. Yet, she also must bear the weight of her own darkened thoughts. Thoughts of revenge, malice and spite are things that meld into heaven's reality. They shape the energy around you. There resides the power of creation in every thought which, if errant, must be cleansed from the soul. These thoughts are terrible masters."

"It seems to me that the father was the one so twisted he could hide behind a corkscrew. He is the one who should be condemned, not Mary," I chimed, feeling much aggrieved at Mary's harsh treatment at his hands.

"And so it is that he atones for his transgressions according to the laws of heaven. He is passed from earth and, even as we speak, is cast into a cauldron where only fierce spirits gnaw at his soul. He is yet in denial to his wrongdoing, captured as he is within the prison of his self-righteousness."

"Will she yet be brought to God?" asked Isaiah in earnest.

"Trying to bring her to God is a contradiction in terms," replied Elijah as he re-joined us. "You cannot bring someone to where they already are."

"How does she fare? She has recouped her energies?" I asked as he sat next to us.

"She is well. She now sleeps and the rest will see her to rejuvenation in due course."

"But how long will it take?"

"The length of her journey of repose is a matter between her and her Father. She is in good hands, fear not."

The quiet magnificence of the vista seemed to still our minds somewhat as our conversation fell to silence. It was both a pleasure and a pain to hear nothing but, well, nothing. It was a pleasure because it gave our minds a chance to sit in repose with itself. A pain because eventually, it had to be broken. Again, it was Isaiah who gave voice to his internal rumblings.

"My friends, I cannot help but give thanks to our Father that my thoughts are now far-removed from earth's strictures."

I looked at him curiously, trying to unscramble his meaning.

"On earth, I was taught that when we die, we either dance with the angels or burn in the pits of hellfire for eternity. I have now seen how far removed my beliefs were from any semblance of truth, grace be to God."

"Such doctrines continue to obstruct our communication with those on earth in need of His tender words," said Elijah in response. "But, have no fear, the truth will not be denied. It will ultimately prevail."

"Yet, man, in his ignorance, still attaches importance to those things that can rightly be 'Rendered to Caesar,'" I added.

It was Atticus who had the final word, as he was compelled to rise and go to Mary when she appeared, standing calm and recovered in the doorway. "Yet these erroneous ideas of man will only delay, they cannot prevent, the ultimate revelation of His truth."

We all, then, rose as one to Mary, with smiles from the heart and love in our hands for her recuperation.

Chapter Fifteen

The Rescues

Across the veil, let us go,
Come, see how.
Abide me, I will show you,
The ease with which it is done.

Abide in Me, heed My words as key,
I am here, my brother.
Lament not, lose not thy faith,
Open your spiritual eyes to see.

Let not a closed mind bar your way,
Let us away.
To rescue we must avail,
So a young soul does not fall prey.

Sometimes, we can,
Others' we cannot.
Innocence the key,
Despair not, however, it is ever this way.

I could barely restrain my urgings to learn. The grand library held such knowledge that I spent many eternal moments reading, delving and absorbing myself with so many tomes of wisdom and knowledge. I was aware that, for his part, Isaiah spent his presence at the school of guardians, learning of the many facets of guardianship, or should I say, 'guardian-angelship'.

When our urgings became irresistible, we would reconvene and share much that we had learned at our respective venues. It must also be said that we were both in gratitude to meet many new acquaintances on our journey. Many who now are considered as kin and able to share spirit and vocation when the thought or need arises.

It was at one such meeting, when in repose at the site of our favoured willow, that Isaiah spoke of his burgeoning desire.

"My friend, I feel full to the brim of love and compassion from all that I have most recently seen and learned. Perhaps it is time to place our feet upon the path to assist those on earth who might benefit from such knowledge?"

"I too feel as you do. Much has been our learning, but this knowledge has no force unless applied to the benefit of others."

"No truer words have been spoken," said Adiel, as he suddenly appeared from behind a nearby tree. "Your wisdom grows as do these very trees," he said in admiration of the same.

It was wonderful to see the grand soul, and our spirit of reacquaintance was not at all masked by veneer.

"You speak of your desire to venture forth with your rucksack full to replete of goodness, I believe," he said to us both similarly. "I come then bearing the fruit of your desire. Yet, I ask that, Athar, you hold fast to your earnestness, for I would take Isaiah first to a place where his love and compassion will best be served to a brother in pressing need."

A fleeting look of disappointment must have passed my visage, for he spoke well to my comfort. "Fear not, my friend, soon, upon our return, will be opportune for you to spread your wings to fly."

"I will attend your return presently," I said to both, "and will send you both forth on the wings of love and angel's breath to light your way."

Then, as the thought was all it took, both Adiel and Isaiah flew to their purpose; I knew not where, but followed them with a light that would secure their passage.

In his small, confined chamber, Brother Isaac was much in

lament. Prostrate on the floor covered only by a threadbare mat, his forehead appeared raw from its abrasions upon the coarse material. From our point of vantage, his eyes were puffy and reddened by the tears that rode down his cheeks in cascade. The small cross hanging from the wall seemed his principal point of focus as he poured his shattered heart towards the object of his desire.

"I have tried, Father. Sorely, I have tried. Yet my faith shakes like the leaves of a tree in a tempest. I do not know what to do. Help me please, I pray of You."

It was hard for Isaiah not to rush to his side and offer comfort to his distress, yet Adiel cautioned his approach with a handclasp firmly to his arm.

"Watch carefully. The time is not quite nigh."

Isaiah could understand his words but could not discern the depths of their wisdom in delay. Yet, he did as was bidden before Adiel's greater understanding of unfolding events. Eventually, Brother Isaac rose from his prone position, wiped his cheeks with his kerchief and moved to sit in the one solitary, comfortless chair to open his grand book of instruction. Isaiah watched carefully as he turned to a dog-eared page. It was to the words of Saint John that he turned, in his search for comfort and the means to surpass his misery. He reread the words aloud many times, and now tried to open his heart to their wisdom:

If ye abide in me, and my words abide in you, ask ye what you will, and it shall be done unto you.
John XV:7

And

This is my commandment. That ye love one another, as I have loved you.
John XV:12

Adiel released Isaiah's arm and motioned that he should move forward. At first tentative, he moved forward to where Isaac sat and sought the words to illuminate his soul. Even to now, Isaiah is unsure of their source, but he spoke from the heart to ears that were opened by anguish.

"Dear Brother, Brother Isaac, it is I, your bish... I mean, Isaiah. I am here," he said speaking in his ear, but as if to his heart. "I told you I would come when your need was great."

Isaiah watched carefully as Isaac sat upright and looked about as if someone were present, but not seeing anyone, he shrugged and cast his gaze back to the Good Book.

"Isaac," he persisted. "It is I, Isaiah," he repeated. But this time he moved his hand to Isaac's fevered brow and touched his forehead with a soft, cooling touch. Again, Isaac's eyes were distracted from his reading, and it was plain to see his hand move involuntarily to his brow as if to acknowledge the cool sensation of Isaiah's touch. Then he seemed to remember...

"My Bishop, is that you?" he said aloud. "Are you here?"

"Yes, it is I, dear friend," Isaiah replied earnestly, as he cast an encouraging glance across to Adiel who watched in calm supervision of the events unfolding.

"I know you are here, my Bishop. I, I can feel your presence, yet my eyes cannot see you."

With his crossed brows deeper than ever, Isaiah made to cause one of the pages of the open book to ruffle slightly, despite the absence of breeze. Isaac's eyes seemed to acknowledge the fact as he held his hands in the position of grace.

"Read the words again, my friend. But this time close your eyes. Read not with your literal or liturgical eyes. Rather, read with your spiritual eyes..." he said, as he watched Isaac close his eyes, not quite hearing the words but feeling their intent. Isaiah watched with a smile as Isaac mouthed the sacred words silently by rote.

"What now do you see? How does your heart direct you?

What would love do next?" Isaiah whispered to his ear.

Isaiah watched carefully as the words seemed to register first in Isaac's heart, then on his face. Placing the Good Book aside and standing to full height and replete breath, his exhale saw him open the door to his chambers and move steadfastly down the hallway. His passage took him via circuitous route up many stairs, but eventually, he arrived at his destination. Whereby he knocked earnestly upon the door. The sign on the door had a different bishop's name, but that was considered only to be expected.

"Enter," came the response from within.

Isaac's hand was steady on the knob that opened the portal, as both Adiel and Isaiah watched close by. Closing the door behind him, they could hear the discourse as it unfolded.

"Bishop," said Isaac, "I come to report a grave injustice to members of our Parish. I have learned much in the confessional that burdens my soul. I would not have it so... Our children are sacred and must stand protected and exalted in His eyes. I would see the correction of such injustice..."

Both Adiel and Isaiah had seen and heard enough. They knew that it was time to return across the veil. Their job had been done, and Isaiah knew forthwith that with an open heart and fierce desire, Brother Isaac's tasks ahead would be many, but filled with promise. Feeling the wind swish across their faces, Adiel and Isaiah drifted over the mists. Their smiles were bright when they saw me standing in attendance, or pacing up and down, as the case may be, waiting impatiently for their return.

It was not necessary to ask how events passed for my friends after they returned. The look upon their faces spoke as much about exhilaration as it did exhaustion. I guessed rightly that a period of repose was needed for both Adiel, and particularly Isaiah, to replenish their stocks of divine energy. This all notwithstanding my impatience to see springboard to similar eventualities.

"Adiel," I asked eventually, "how is it that many on earth do not hold account of the continued efforts of the spirit world to enlighten their path through the adversity of life?"

"A closed mind to the truth is like the bars of a cell holding a prisoner enthralled. These bars, as we have much discussed, can be imposed by errors and limitations of errant doctrine or conditioning. They can also be caused by fear. Fear of the unknown. Fear of what lies beyond the five senses of the earthly domain, and, more abundantly, the fear of 'not being worthy in the eyes of our Father'. Fear that they may not 'measure up' to the aspirations of God's eternal decrees. After having been told so often that they are 'sinners', it is often hard to recognise one's divinity."

"I stand guilty as charged," intoned Isaiah as he raised his voice from his respite.

"And with the dawn of truth, dear Isaiah, have not your eyes now been opened to the majesty of heaven's abode?"

"Oh, indeed! My eyes have been firmly opened to His domain, never to be again closed to His love."

"Yet how shall I proclaim such majesty?" said I in deference to my eagerness to spread goodwill upon those in need.

Adiel's crinkled smile said that he understood my meaning and rose to my urgings.

"Yes, my friend, I hear your entreat. It is time to venture on such exploration as your soul fervently desires. But I caution to temper your exuberance with the knowledge that not always do our desired outcomes meet our expectations."

He looked at me closely to ensure my understanding, as I tried to temper my enthusiasm for the task behind my eyes masked in deference to his wisdom.

"Let us away then," he said, taking a firm hold around my waist. "We shall presently return, dear Isaiah. Fear not for our safe return, for we are comforted by the hand of God's grace to our travails ahead."

We found ourselves in a hallway of hyperactivity. The bell summoned the many classes to be dismissed at once and the throng of student bodies filled the hallway, intent on the outside area of recreation. I do confess that if it were not for Adiel's steadying hand, I would have found it a great challenge to remain amidst the excitement of such errant energies. Yet, Adiel stood firm to his purpose. So, we waited. What we were waiting for, I could not quite determine, but I watched him watching carefully.

I could see from our perched view above the throng, that standing among the many exiting mass of students was a master in attendance of their proper behaviour. He seemed resolute to task with hands placed behind his back and his eyes peeled on and through the mass of young bodies. He seemed none too perturbed by the noise, yet, somehow, he seemed to resonate an aura of authority mixed with malice. It was as if his radiated energy betrayed his deeper thoughts. His aura was as dark as his habit.

As my attention was closely watching the overseer, I failed to see Adiel move as swiftly as a cat upon his intended prey. I turned suddenly to see him approach a young boy. A boy in earthly terms of tender years. He seemed rather morose, and none too captured by others' eager desire to participate in sport or lively banter. He trailed behind the others, walking slowly. Adiel was by his side in an instant. I could hear his entreat even without listening. "Hurry, hurry," he seemed to say, imploring the youth to take hastened steps.

I watched closely at what was occurring and struggled to ascertain my role in the events unfolding. Then I saw him move. The wolf was intent upon his quarry. I saw him move towards the youth as his aura dripped with a darkened hue. It was exactly then I knew what to do. I saw it first, even before he did. The water spilt from the bottle from a student's careless intent made the stone floor a little slippery. I couldn't resist, even now though, I do not know how I managed it. Perhaps it was the surging heat that rose suddenly in my being. Perhaps, it was rage, or maybe an overpowering desire to see harm averted. But the gentle nudge applied to the priest's shoulder was enough to see him slip in the offending puddle and topple over to his knees. I guess he must have hurt himself, but I'm certain it was not to the extreme. Although I did notice no one came to his aid.

Adiel turned briefly from his intent with a half-smile, still imploring his charge to further speed towards the outside area of play whereby the attention of other guardians would be more intent to his proper welfare.

Later, as we three reconvened under our favoured willow, it was Adiel who spoke of our successful intervention.

"Sometimes, when the conditions are to our favour – when the innocence of youth shines brightly, it is ever possible for us to intervene against darkness. Many other times, most unfortunately, it does not..."

I looked at my mentor with eyes that reflected the depths of my gratitude. But I knew there was much more to be done.

Chapter Sixteen

The Chosen Pathway

Never the weary travellers are we,
Fired by purpose divine.
Time in heaven knows no bounds,
Eternity spreads across our domain.

But attend thee now,
Face the final hurdle, you must.
Her fate entwined with thine,
You are yet God's divine hand.

Watch, first see,
The power of the divine at play.
Her fate unfolds by deeds of her own hands,
Clothed in rags of darkness.

My heart trembles, to burst asunder,
Mother am I to you, do as I say.
Nay, no more – that is enough!
I forgive you, but accept it, you cannot.

As unfolded events have preceded, both Isaiah and I were
acutely aware that much has been realised. We had made the
crossover through the veil many times. We had both secured
success and known the bitterness of defeat. For his part, Isaiah
had seen much errant doctrine cast to the nether for devout
souls with the ears to hear. He had witnessed the blossom of
truth in the hearts of many. Those who were before shackled by
words directed from the pulpit that played scant resemblance to
the forest of heaven's vast realities.

For me, I had ministered many calming words to those who suffered under the yoke of persecution and misguided power. It was particularly pleasing for me to know that many amongst the succoured were children of tender and innocent age. Yet, we were both aware that much more remained. Too many of our words fell upon closed ears or were deafened by the force of temptation for earthly allures.

"We have realised many things, have we not, my dear friend," I said to Isaiah as we sat in recline upon the balcony of my abode. "If I cast my mind back from when we began, I have trouble assimilating the wonder of our progress. Yet I fear there is much more to do."

"It is most fortunate that time runs to eternity in heaven, Athar, otherwise we would be short of the precious gift of its implementation," he said as he lolled leisurely on the chaise lounge.

"You speak the truth, but if I know of heaven's laws, then one is certain to remain in a constant progress of evolution."

"I, for one, am happy to remain in service to whatever need should arise from the palm of His hand..." I vowed earnestly, before being truncated by the vibrations of a silver cord that appeared suddenly and without expectation upon my chest. Although startled, I knew exactly what the calling was. I looked at Isaiah solemnly. He knew my mind and was instantly alert to its implications.

"Would you like me to attend by your side, dear friend? I could be much to your service with such a pressing responsibility."

"I will be forever grateful for your assistance and comfort by my side," I confirmed as I nodded my intent by which we should proceed.

The journey to the point of necessity was swift but by no means without trepidation. I became even more comforted by Isaiah's presence when we reached the hilltop overlooking the exit portal.

The mists seemed no less opaque than my previous recollections and the constant stream of souls exiting the door was ever the wonder to behold. As is always the case, many were the designated beings-of-light here to minister to those who had recently crossed over. So many exiting the portal were in a state of malady. Many crippled by life's errant journey or confused about their current whereabouts. Yet, some appeared replete with joy at the transition and were greeted as such by kin and loved ones previously departed.

I looked earnestly among the fold of souls but only needed to follow the silver cord's progression. She was standing, confused, but resolute to the side of the road that led from the portal of the mists. I could discern, even from a distance, the haughty nature of her posture, the self-indulged smile that fixed to her lips but which remained absent from her eyes.

I made fast to walk towards her, but for some reason unknown, Isaiah held my arm fast, as if to say, not yet, my friend. Watch! Wait!

She was greeted by one of the blessed attendants tasked with the comfort of those who recently arrived. I could see her scant regard for the care and concern she received. I could see her remonstration at the colouration of her garment. The dull greyish-brown hessian mixed with sharp flashes of black did in no way treat her outlook with the sensibility she considered her station. Despite her vehement protestations, the attendant persisted in his efforts to calm her insecurities. Both Isaiah and I could see his erstwhile efforts to direct her along the pathway of her designation. Yet, she brushed aside such concern and strode purposely forward, seeking a road that she believed better suited to her state of expectation.

We watched in earnest as she strode towards a pathway leading upwards and towards a higher domain. The colours of the pathway in no way matching the distinctive colour of her attire. Although making effort to engage, she was ignored by the many others who streamed by and by. Yet she persisted until she could progress no further. It was as if she was confronted by a brick wall but could not see any means by which she was retarded. Frustrated yet determined, she retraced her steps to try another, but the same result ensued. Then she tried another, then another, until such time as her determination waned to the inevitable. It was then the moment of my greatest trial. I moved forward to her aid as she stood before the dank pathway of her realisation.

"Mother," I said, approaching from down the hillslope and trying hard to hold fast to all of that which I had learnt in love. She turned abruptly at my approach.

"Help get these things off me," she said in curt entreat as she made exerted effort to rend her garment from her shoulders. "I don't deserve this! I should be treated with more respect. Look at this trash..."

Then she seemed to notice my attire. The multifaceted hues and vibrant colours emanating from within my being.

"Look at you," she said with a sneer. "How is it that you are clothed so, and I am dressed in such miserable fashion. Who do you think you are? You're no better than I. You shouldn't be dressed like that. Go and do something about it! Who's in charge here? I want to see someone important."

It took some exerted effort to remain stoic in the face of such a torrent. I could feel my body shake under my robe and I was hopeful that my eyes did not betray my sense of unease in the face of her 'force majeure'.

"I can do nothing for these robes, Mother. They are the determination within the mists and may never be rendered asunder."

Her look of disdain for my words was like a sword thrust to the heart. "Do as I say. Find me someone in authority. You are evidently no more valuable now than you were back then. Forever in my way. Forever under my feet. You're useless."

It came like a thunderbolt and without sign or warning. I felt the heat pierce my heart like a spear from heaven.

"No more! That's enough," I said with more angst and animation than I could ever recall having portrayed. "Your disdain for others has come to an end. You are my mother, and may the records show that I will forever be blessed by the union. For without such trial, I would not be wearing the garb of light with which I am now attired."

I must confess, in hindsight I had never spoken to my mother in such a fashion, as much as I had never seen her so stunned. Her mouth dropped open at my tone and my words seemed to echo to the core of her being... so I continued.

"You have lived your life in total disregard for others. You have hurt people with intent. You have destroyed every relationship that was ever placed before you by grace. What you have sown, so shall you now reap. This is the law so affixed by God. The consequences are now yours for eternity."

Yes, my words did pierce, and I watched as tears formed to their reality. But I knew this also to be a façade... so I continued.

"Follow this pathway, you will. In the darkness of fear shall you abide, until..." I said until I hesitated.

"Until what?" she replied, wiping the crocodile tears from her eyes.

"Until you can accept the forgiveness I have offered. From my hand or another's, you will eventually see the light which it brings. I am your kin, your son, I forgive you. Yet, you no more see the love from my hand, as you can from that offered by our loving-Father. Be gone now. I will attend to you no more! Only I will be ever here when the light breaks through the deep crusts of your self-absorption. Know that as justice weighs its yoke upon your shoulders, I will be here to unlock the latch... When your knees no longer bear the weight, and you are upon them."

I could see she was crestfallen. Somehow my words had broken through. I knew not how deeply, nor to what extent they had cut. Yet, I could tell from the downcast slump of her shoulders how she had become resigned to her fate. She turned to look down the road of her construction and, unlike before, she was not impeded in her progress.

Seeing her thus, I was almost ready to shout after her that her judgement was neither eternal nor vindictive. But, once again and thankfully, Isaiah was by my side to place a restraining hand to my lips.

"Those words would not help at this stage, my brother. Wisdom such as this can only be heard by those with ears to hear. When the light of our Father's love shines through the crack you have made to her darkness."

I was never so comforted by my friend's presence as he helped me with care back to my place of abode.

Chapter Seventeen

The Great Vista

Grand Master, such grace do I now see,
The wonders of the seven laying before me.
Such music divine,
Such colours unknown to mine eyes.

Love forever will be our bond,
Let it light your way.
Behold that which I AM,
Of heaven and earth am I.

Be not in earnest,
Love thy brother as thyself.
Then you will see,
The bounty, the love before thee.

Love you I do, forever unto day,
Separate we are not, this cannot be.
Come, abide with me,
Tarry not, for eternity awaits.

I do not remember how long it was. All I recall is being handled gently onto the reclining lounge at my home with Isaiah standing by in sentinel. I know he sat holding my hand with the care of heaven and soothing my soul with words of comfort and ease. My sleep of rest did not avail dreams. Dreams are not a necessity of the repose of heaven. Rather, I felt the clouds enfold me in a feeling of abject peace and eternal love. I seemed to drift through the ethers where only the divine hand played music of exquisite cadence and symphony – I know not for what duration.

When my eyes opened, I was greeted with an array of beaming smiles. Not only was Isaiah still by my side, but also to attendance were both Elijah and Atticus... and the Master. I could barely restrain my eagerness to rise from my recline, but the Master lay a gentle, but firm hand upon my shoulder, imploring me to remain in repose.

"You have come to great enlightenment, my dear Athar," he said with both his words and the depths of his compassion through his eyes. "Your service before the lord of Hosts has been anointed to His glory, and so shall it ever be writ upon the records."

As if in chorale, the others intoned, "Amen."

"I, I am here only by His grace, Master," I managed to stammer. "My road has been no more troubled than many travelled before me."

"Spoken like a true child of the divine," noted Atticus from the side of the recliner.

"Perhaps it is time that you told him your news," said the Master, looking up at Atticus with a glint in his eye.

"News! What news? There are more surprises?" I said, stunned to full awakening as I rose to sit upright.

Atticus cleared his throat and stood tall as if to claim the attention that was already his. All eyes fell to his declaration.

"From across the ages have you ever been in my heart, dear Athar. I have been by your side since the day that your soul was quickened in the womb. Ever cradled by my hands to comfort you were, as you traversed the redemptive fire of your life. Your every pain and endured suffering I felt like my own. But now, you are here as one with me and all our kindred in the cradle of our Father's arms. It has been a grand journey and one befitting such a soul with stature such as yours."

"I, I don't. I don't know what to say..."

Then the Master came forward. Immediately, it was as if the

light in the chamber had ignited with the very touch of bliss.

"Together, forever will be your bond, dear Athar. For Atticus in your earthly life was your grandfather. The grandfather that loved you from the day your eyes opened to the sun. Such love that you have, one for the other, will never be diminished so long as your souls abide its beauty."

I could barely restrain the surge to my affection. I did not have to, for the warmth of our embrace was like the sun and the stars in eternal accord. My tears flowed unhindered by thoughts of contrition or blush. I was home – where never before I had been.

Much was our merry and joyous revelry. All until the Master deemed the moment just right, when he held his hands outstretched. We each knew that his forthcoming words were replete with all the power of love in his possession.

"Athar and Isaiah, I believe it is now time to show you further the vast expanse of our Father's domain of heaven. Your trials have been many, yet now, shown to you will be a vista spoken of only in supplication and prayers of faith. Do you choose to see that which is still to become?"

I was almost too overawed to find a proper voice to affirm my intent. I was even hesitant to glance towards Isaiah for fear of his refusal, but all those inane thoughts disappeared when the Master again spoke.

"Good, it is settled. Let us away, then." To Atticus and Elijah, he spoke solemnly before our departure. "My brothers, we shall presently return, and with God's full grace, I thank you for the loving care you have bestowed upon both Athar and Isaiah across their journey."

A humble nod of acknowledgement was all that was required from our two mentors before the Master clasped us both firmly around the waist, and, with the speed of thought we were away.

I can vividly recall the waves of resistance that seemed to melt before the Master's presence. Watching everything with a keen eye for recollection meant that I could barely avert my gaze from the wonder. Isaiah was also so engrossed by the same experience. I did, however, manage to cast a glance at our guardian's face as we sped across the ethers. It was a visage that spoke of the radiance of love. If ever love was defined as a power, it would be in reflection of what his eyes spoke as truth. Thereby, we alighted. I cannot say for certain whether it was to the crest of a magnificent mountain, or perhaps an outlook from a point fixed only by the stars. But of one thing I am certain – that what we saw defied all before it in sheer majesty. No view upon the earth could ever come close to that which Isaiah and I now bore witness.

As we alighted from the transportation, both Isaiah and I stood for an eternity while the scene before us unfolded to its grandeur. The Master, standing between us, remained content for us to behold the never to be forgotten. It was as if we could see the whole. The entirety of the kingdom of heaven lay open before us to be viewed with eyes awed with veneration. It took some eternal moments for me to find a voice in search of words to both describe the wonder, then ask the myriad of questions that were beginning to form in a logjam. Although it must be said, the Master did seem to know my heart before a voice could be found.

"When your eyes can bear the glory, is when you will see its majesty," he proclaimed, watching us both carefully.

I should begin to describe to you what we saw, and I trust that my friend Isaiah can add to that which may only be supplied by me in limitation. I will begin first with the colours. If one could imagine the rainbows of earth multiplied and magnified, such that the depth and hues of the seven paints were but a minuscule representation of the ocean from which these colours were drawn. Then you would see what I see. These colours pervaded everything that lay before us. From top to bottom, for inside and out. All, everything, was colour. From across, to through the seven heavens, these multi-hues imbued everything and all from within. From the highest peaks to the greatest depths – it was not light, it was colour. The colour was light.

Standing above and beyond us was a golden glow, so bright that it almost blinded the eye to regard. Then, looking down to the nether regions, it was entirely possible to see the golden light still a glow, but overshadowed. It was from the depths of darkness that seemed to exude from the souls present within. Yet, the golden glow was ever-present. It was as if the evil and base thoughts and deeds of man, captured by sin, had smeared a thick veneer over the golden light, now opaque and oft impossible to see. Where the yoke of guilt lay heavily upon the soul, did the glorious colours of heaven stay muted to its ever-presence. "Oh, Master," I intoned, "if man could only see what I am blessed to see. If only he knew that by opening his heart to the awareness of God's spirit, would he too see the majestic nature of the gifts that have been showered upon him."

"Yes, dear Athar, salvation lies within never an absence of divine light, just an inability to see it. Yet, the needs of every soul, without exception, are carefully discerned and ministered to in preparation for their evolvement. God would have all men be saved."

Then there was the music. The music, like a stream of divine mist, infused all that it touched. It was the most beautiful sound I had ever heard. A hundred, a thousand musicians played a never-ending sonata, rending the heart with violin and harp in joyous accord. It touched all, it felt all and was remiss to nothing and no one. The grasses sang to its joy. The trees praised its presence and swayed in cadence to its rhythm. They could hear it. It was the music that infused the crocus and acorn with their knowing how to grow to flower and rainforest. It was the gentle rhyme that told the story of our Father's eternal love.

Yet, I saw that man had not the ears to hear. Deaf to the minims and maxims were those that sought to impose their will and control over the notes.

"Let go, let God," spoke the words from the melody. "Seek and ye shall find," proclaimed another verse. "I am here, I have always been. Abide in me," cried the next stanza.

"When you build your foundations with His word, your castle will have His cornerstones. Yet, those who seek to create an edifice of power and greed bereft of concern for his fellowman, will crumble to dust – they too shall fall," spoke the Master.

"How? When, Master? When will they hear the music?" asked Isaiah in earnest.

"In the quiet between each inhale and exhale of breath. When the mind ceases to seek control. When the heart is rent open to let the music in – then will all ears be attuned to His grace. Let me in, let me in, proclaims His word. My love awaits."

I watched as I saw the musical cadence drift unheard past the ears of so many. Yet, some heard the call from within. Many who stood still to listen. I saw an army of souls ready to abide by His every calling.

"You and I are one – abide in me," was the calling. "Ask of me what you will, and it shall be done unto you."

I could not help it. I fell to my knees before the majesty before me. Tears flowed, not as pain or relief, but as a joyous reunion with He who has been with me all along. I reached for Isaiah's hand to give thanks for our journey to eternity and I heard his voice cherish our union.

"Do you see the seven heavens, dear Isaiah? We are truly blessed, we two."

"Yes, we are," he replied. "And now we have much more to proclaim to His wonder, do we not?"

"Indeed, we do, my friend. Indeed, we do."

I wasn't sure how or how long was our return. But by the time my eyes beheld the surrounds of my abode, I was unconscious of how I had arrived. With a start did I open my eyes and was ever glad to see Isaiah in repose next to me. He too seemed to be in recovery from bliss. When he finally opened his eyes, I could barely find a word to ask of his well-being, although I could see in his eyes the reflection of my own.

"What now, my friend?" I asked after he rose from his recline.

"I do not know," he said. "Perhaps we better ask God."

A very good suggestion, I thought.

Epilogue

It should come as no surprise, that for me, the writing of this book was a pleasure in the unfolding. Yet, pleasure does not fully account for the wonder that was experienced. Grateful, I am. Thankful to the core of my being, for the grace shown by spirits willing to pierce my soul with the words that have been given to light these pages.

Yet, the journey is not mine alone. You now, having read these words, have been presented with the grandest opportunity. The opportunity to realise the truth of your divine essence. The spark within you now blossoms to fire. A fire not of destruction, but light and colour. A light that creates love and wisdom. The seal has been broken. The latch upon the closed chest is now open. You have the key. No more barriers, no more hesitation. NOW becomes the time for the full expression of your greatest version.

Do not wait! Do not tarry! The time is now ripe. Inside, you know what you have to do. Your truth speaks to you in cascade. Let such truth speak not just to whisper but to volume. Never absent, always to the ready. Do not wait for crisis or tears. The time to listen is NOW.

Stop. Listen. Breathe deep. Between the inhale and the exhale is the point of wonder between the two. This is when the voice can be heard. Try it! Even when all is agog around you. Especially when all is agog around you. There you will find in discovery the words sought to your comfort. The inspiration to spark you to a higher calling or turned from errant temptation.

As has been said throughout this story, that "God would have all men be saved." Let us not, therefore, delay in such regard. All time is relative to our experience of the divine, not the revolutions of the sun.

Let it be so!

**6TH
BOOKS**

ALL THINGS PARANORMAL

Investigations, explanations and deliberations on the paranormal,
supernatural, explainable or unexplainable. 6th Books seeks to
give answers while nourishing the soul: whether making use of the
scientific model or anecdotal and fun, but always
beautifully written.
Titles cover everything within parapsychology: how to, lifestyles,
alternative medicine, beliefs, myths and theories.
If you have enjoyed this book, why not tell other readers by
posting a review on your preferred book site?

Recent bestsellers from 6th Books are:

The Afterlife Unveiled
What the Dead Are Telling us About Their World!
Stafford Betty
What happens after we die? Spirits speaking through mediums
know, and they want us to know. This book unveils their world...
Paperback: 978-1-84694-496-3 ebook: 978-1-84694-926-5

Spirit Release
Sue Allen
A guide to psychic attack, curses, witchcraft, spirit attachment,
possession, soul retrieval, haunting, deliverance, exorcism and
more, as taught at the College of Psychic Studies.
Paperback: 978-1-84694-033-0 ebook: 978-1-84694-651-6

I'm Still With You
True Stories of Healing Grief Through Spirit Communication
Carole J. Obley
A series of after-death spirit communications which uplift, comfort
and heal, and show how love helps us grieve.
Paperback: 978-1-84694-107-8 ebook: 978-1-84694-639-4

Less Incomplete
A Guide to Experiencing the Human Condition Beyond the
Physical Body
Sandie Gustus
Based on 40 years of scientific research, this book is a dynamic
guide to understanding life beyond the physical body.
Paperback: 978-1-84694-351-5 ebook: 978-1-84694-892-3

Advanced Psychic Development
Becky Walsh
Learn how to practise as a professional, contemporary spiritual medium.
Paperback: 978-1-84694-062-0 ebook: 978-1-78099-941-8

Astral Projection Made Easy
and overcoming the fear of death
Stephanie June Sorrell
From the popular Made Easy series, *Astral Projection Made Easy* helps to eliminate the fear of death, through discussion of life beyond the physical body.
Paperback: 978-1-84694-611-0 ebook: 978-1-78099-225-9

The Miracle Workers Handbook
Seven Levels of Power and Manifestation of the Virgin Mary
Sherrie Dillard
Learn how to invoke the Virgin Mary's presence, communicate with her, receive her grace and miracles and become a miracle worker.
Paperback: 978-1-84694-920-3 ebook: 978-1-84694-921-0

Divine Guidance
The Answers You Need to Make Miracles
Stephanie J. King
Ask any question and the answer will be presented, like a direct line to higher realms… *Divine Guidance* helps you to regain control over your own journey through life.
Paperback: 978-1-78099-794-0 ebook: 978-1-78099-793-3

The End of Death
How Near-Death Experiences Prove the Afterlife
Admir Serrano
A compelling examination of the phenomena of Near-Death
Experiences.
Paperback: 978-1-78279-233-8 ebook: 978-1-78279-232-1

Where After
Mariel Forde Clarke
A journey that will compel readers to view life after death in a
completely different way.
Paperback: 978-1-78904-617-5 ebook: 978-1-78904-618-2

Harvest: The True Story of Alien Abduction
G L Davies
G. L. Davies's most terrifying investigation yet reveals one
woman's terrifying ordeal of alien visitation, nightmarish visions
and a prophecy of destruction on a scale never before seen in
Pembrokeshire's peaceful history.
Paperback:978-1-78904-385-3 ebook: 978-1-78904-386-0

The Scars of Eden
Paul Wallis
How do we distinguish between our ancestors' ideas of God and
close encounters of an extra-terrestrial kind?
Paperback: 978-1-78904-852-0 ebook: 978-1-78904-853-7

Readers of ebooks can buy or view any of these bestsellers by clicking on the live link in the title. Most titles are published in paperback and as an ebook. Paperbacks are available in traditional bookshops. Both print and ebook formats are available online.
Find more titles and sign up to our readers' newsletter at http://www.johnhuntpublishing.com/mind-body-spirit.
Follow us on Facebook at https://www.facebook.com/OBooks and Twitter at https://twitter.com/obooks.